中国人民革命军事博物馆 编

制胜之道

THE PATH TO VICTORY

孙子兵法暨中国古代军事文物精品展

The Exhibition of The Art of War and Fine Antiques of Ancient Chinese Military

文物出版社

封面设计　周小玮
责任印制　陆　联
责任编辑　赵　磊　李　诤

图书在版编目（CIP）数据

制胜之道：孙子兵法暨中国古代军事文物精品展/中国
人民革命军事博物馆编.—北京：文物出版社，2008.7
ISBN 978-7-5010-2537-4

Ⅰ.制... Ⅱ.中... Ⅲ.①孙子兵法-研究②军事-历史
文物-中国-古代　Ⅳ.E 892.25　K875.804

中国版本图书馆CIP数据核字（2008）第104645号

制胜之道
——孙子兵法暨中国古代军事文物精品展

编　　者　中国人民革命军事博物馆
出版发行　文物出版社
地　　址　北京市东直门内北小街2号楼
　　　　　100007
　　　　　http://www.wenwu.com
　　　　　web@wenwu.com

制版印刷　北京燕泰美术制版印刷有限责任公司
经　　销　新华书店
版　　次　2008年7月第1版第1次印刷
开　　本　889×1194　　1/16
印　　张　11.5
ISBN 978-7-5010-2537-4

定　　价　160.00元

制胜之道
孙子兵法暨中国古代军事文物精品展

主办单位

中国人民革命军事博物馆

北京市文物局

协办单位

安徽省博物馆

安庆市博物馆

河北省文物研究所

湖北省博物馆

荆州博物馆

河南博物院

河南省文物考古研究所

南阳市文物考古研究所

湖南省博物馆

内蒙古自治区博物馆

山东省博物馆

银雀山汉墓竹简博物馆

齐国故城遗址博物馆

陕西历史博物馆

陕西省考古研究所

咸阳市博物馆

昭陵博物馆

云南省博物馆

昆明市博物馆

浙江省博物馆

《制胜之道——孙子兵法暨中国古代军事文物精品展》

主　编

郭得河　程建国　孔繁峙

副　主　编

佘志宏　郝晓进　舒小峰　于　平

执行编辑

王辉强　黄亦兵

编　辑

李　斌　高玉林　王丽丹　张艳华　陈　琪

图　片

李越英　唐升健　王　钢

翻　译

世纪金信技术翻译

英文校审

邸　峥

展示制胜之道 弘扬优秀文化

在北京奥运会举办之际，中国人民革命军事博物馆、北京市文物局共同主办"制胜之道——孙子兵法暨中国古代军事文物精品展"。这个展览是专门为北京奥运会打造的，目的是为弘扬中华民族优秀传统文化，提高国家文化软实力，丰富北京奥运会期间的社会文化生活。

产生于中国春秋时代晚期的《孙子兵法》，距今已有2500多年历史，是世界现存最古老的兵书，也是迄今为止影响最为持久和深远的军事理论著作，被公认为世界历史上第一个系统的军事理论体系。作为东方智慧的结晶，《孙子兵法》集中体现了中国古代军事思想的极高成就，被誉为"兵学圣典"，在2500多年的军事实践中发挥了重要的指导作用。

将《孙子兵法》这样一部中华文明优秀之作，以展览的形式表现出来，形象化地介绍给广大观众，让更多的人了解这部军事名著，是一件极为有益的事情。特别是在今年的世界体育盛会——北京奥运会举办之际展出，更显得意义重大。因为奥运会不仅是体育的盛会，也是文化的盛会。凡举办奥运会的国家，无不借此机会，大力弘扬民族文化，张显民族性格，展示民族风貌。中华文化源远流长，博大精深，其中许多优秀的思想，不仅没有随时间的推移而湮没，反而愈来愈光芒四射。《孙子兵法》就是如此。它是一部兵书，但宣扬的不是无限暴力，而是慎战思想，即通过"伐谋"、"伐交"等手段，达到"不战而屈人之兵"的目的，实现"兵不顿而利可全"的理想。这与当今世界和平发展的主题是相契合的，也是为什么当今人们重视和推崇它的原因。

这个展览通过经典战例、精品文物和孙子论著诠释，展示《孙子兵法》博大精深的军事思想，揭示它何以历久弥新、由军事领域贯通到人类社会活动多个领域的奥秘。展览以展示《孙子兵法》思想精髓为主题，以军事历史发展阶段为脉络，以古代军事文物精品为主体，辅以相关的历史图片、模型、艺术品等。在内容设计和展品选择时，充分运用国内外对孙子兵法的研究成果，突出中华民族特色，充分考虑国外观众对中华民族文化的认知度和欣赏点，在内容精致、准确的基础上增强观赏性。

这次展览得到国内20家博物馆和文物考古研究部门大力支持，提供了近60件（套）古代军事文物。它们齐聚京城，可让兵器及文物爱好者大饱眼福。这批文物中不乏享誉中外的国宝。如银雀山汉墓竹简、曾侯乙墓出土的三戈戟、云南博物馆的汉代战争场面储贝器盖、湖南博物馆的西汉驻军图等。特别是一些与孙子有关的春秋吴越两国的文物，如湖北博物馆的春秋越王勾践剑、浙江博物馆的战国州句越王剑、安徽博物馆的春秋吴太子姑发剑、安庆市博物馆的战国越王丌北古剑等，代表着春秋战国时期精湛的铸剑水平，凝聚着两国之间及与其他诸侯国争雄的历史。它们平时散处于各省博物馆，如今借孙子兵法展的契机，会聚一堂，对于广大观众来说，是不可多得的鉴赏机会。

"制胜之道——孙子兵法暨中国古代军事文物精品展"，第一次把《孙子兵法》这样一部带有哲学高度军事理论著作，在国内博物馆界，以展览的形式介绍给广大观众。为了能准确地反映孙子思想，展览集国内研究孙子兵法成果之大成，在大纲起草阶段，吴如嵩研究员、吴九龙研究员、李零教授、任力研究员、刘庆研究员等国内研究孙子兵法的知名专家学者多次予以指导。可以说，没有这些专家学者和其他博物馆的倾力相助，这个展览是难以成功的。在此谨向他们致以谢意。

最后要说的是，"制胜之道——孙子兵法暨中国古代军事文物精品展"，展示的是中国古代优秀的军事文化，弘扬的是"自古知兵非好战"的思想。中华民族是爱好和平的民族，历来主张"不侵大国之地，不耗小国之民"，"不劫人以兵甲，不威人以众强"（《晏子春秋》）。今天，让我们领会《孙子兵法》的思想的精髓，坚持和平发展，促进人类进步，推动建设持久和平、共同繁荣的和谐世界。

中国人民革命军事博物馆馆长　少将

Demonstrating Strategy for Victory Highlighting Brilliant Culture

To herald the Beijing Olympic Games, "The Path to Victory: The Exhibition of The Art of War and Fine Antiques of Ancient Chinese Military" co-organized by the Military Museum of Chinese People's Revolution and Beijing Municipal Administration of Cultural Heritage is now open to the public. The exhibition, specially designed for the Beijing Olympic Games, aims to highlight the brilliant traditional culture of China, enhance Chinese culture as national "soft power", and enrich the socio-cultural life during the Beijing Olympics.

The Art of War with a history of over 2500 years was produced in the later stage of the Spring and Autumn Period (770BC-476BC). Being the oldest military book in the world with the most enduring and profound influence so far, this masterpiece is recognized as the first system of military theory in the world history. As an embodiment of oriental wisdom and a vivid reflection of the brilliant ancient Chinese military thinking, it is credited as "the masterpiece of military strategy", offering significant directions to the military operations over 2500 years.

It's a meaningful endeavor to introduce The Art of War, a masterpiece in Chinese civilization, through a vivid exhibition, making it known by more people. More importantly, the exhibition is held in parallel with Beijing Olympic Games, a world sports feast of 2008. The Olympic Games is not only a grand feast for sports, but also for culture. Every country hosting the Olympic Games takes this chance to promote their national culture, highlight their national character and demonstrate their national style. Chinese culture, extensive and profound, survives a long history. Many great ideas become more conspicuous instead of going oblivion with time and The Art of War is a case in point.

Though it's a military book, what it advocates is cautious attitude toward waging wars rather than unrestrained violence, that is, try to subdue the enemy's army without battle through "attacking the enemy's strategy" and "disrupting the enemy's alliances by diplomacy", so as to realize the ideal of "achieving triumphs without deploying a man". The idea is right in line with the theme of peace and development of present world, which also explains why it has attracted so much attention and has been held so highly now.

The Exhibition unveils the breadth and profoundness of Sun Tzu's military thoughts from diverse dimensions - exemplary ancient and modern battles, select antiques and interpretation of the book. It will reveal what account for its enduring glamour and why it can find applications in fields far beyond the military. Centering on the essence of The Art of war and following the chronological order in the military history, the exhibition is focused on the select ancient military antiques, complemented by the relevant historical pictures, models and artworks. The design of the subjects and selection of antiques largely integrate the relevant academic work by both foreign and domestic researcher. The exhibition not only gives full play to the distinctive feature of the Chinese nation, but also takes into consideration foreign guests perception and aesthetic angle of Chinese culture, thus making it more enjoyable in addition to providing exquisite presentation and accurate information.

The exhibiton features 60 (piece/set) ancient military antiques offered by 20 museums and research institutes of culture heritage and archeology in China. Collectively on display in Beijing, they will be a feast to the lovers of weapons and antiques. You can find among these items on display a number of national treasures which enjoy a world fame, such as the bamboo slips excavated from the Tomb of Han Dynasty in Yinque hill, the ternary halberd excavated from Zenghouyi Tomb, the cover of the Shell Money Storage Container with battle pictures of Western Han Dynasty (Yunnan Provincial Museum), the map of Garrison in Western Han Dynasty (Hunan Provincial Museum) and so on. Particularly, some antiques related to Sun Tzu dated back to State of Wu and the State of Yue in the Spring and Autumn Period, representing the sophisticated sword casting technology at that time and are reminiscent of the struggles for overload between these two countries and among other feudal states, such as the sword of Gou Jian, the King of Yue (Hubei Provincial Museum); the sword of Zhou Gou, the King of Yue, of the Warring States Period (Zhejiang Provincial Museum); the sword of Gu Fa, the princess of Wu in the Spring and Autumn Period (Anhui Provincial Museum) and the sword of Qi Bei, the King of Yue in the Warring State Period (Anqing Municipal Museum). It is a rare opportunity for visitors to appreciate all these antiques, which were scattered in different provincial museums, at the exhibition of The Art of War.

"The Path to Victory: The Exhibition of The Art of War and Fine Antiques of Ancient Chinese Military" is the first to introduce to the visitors a masterpiece on military theory filled with philosophical principles through an exhibition in the national museum. The exhibition integrates the academic work of domestic researchers on The Art of War so as to present accurate information about Sun Tzu's thinking. well-known experts on The Art of War including Researcher Wu Rusong, Researcher Wu Jiulong, Prof. Li Ling, Researcher Ren Li, Researcher Liu Qing have offered guidance many times in drafting the outline of the exhibition. The exhibition wouldn't have been successfully completed without the support of these experts and domestic museums. Hereby we'd like to extend our sincere gratitude to them all.

To conclude, it needs to be emphasized that the exhibition "The Path to Victory: The Exhibition of The Art of War and Fine Antiques of Ancient Chinese Military" aims to unveil the brilliance of ancient Chinese military culture and highlight the idea "carrying out the tradition: grasping the law of war, but not being belligerent". Chinese always love peace, long advocating the idea of "never invading the territory of any large power and never attrit the people of any small nation" (Yan Zi Spring and Autumn Annals). Today, while appreciating the essence of The Art of War, let's stick to maintaining world peace and development, promoting the progress of mankind and contributing to building a harmonious world of lasting peace and common prosperity.

Major General,Curator of the Military Museum of Chinese People's Revolution

前　言
Foreword

　　《孙子兵法》成书于中国春秋（公元前770——前476年）末期，汲取了前人的战争经验，揭示了一系列根本性的军事规律，形成了系统的军事理论，被誉为"兵学圣典"，在2500多年的军事实践中发挥了重要的指导作用。它由古代走向现代、由中国走向世界、由军事战线走向社会其他领域，在世界范围内日益受到广泛关注。为了让更多的人了解这部军事名著，在北京奥运会举办之际，中国人民革命军事博物馆、北京市文物局共同主办"制胜之道——孙子兵法 暨中国古代军事文物精品展"。

　　展览通俗地揭示了《孙子兵法》的思想精髓，汇聚了国内二十家博物馆珍藏的古代军事文物。这些精品文物承载着中国古代军事历史，闪烁着科学技术之光，与军事理论一样，是战争胜利的重要因素，是人类共有的军事文化遗产。

　　The Art of War, completed at the end of the Spring and Autumn Period in Chinese history (770BC—476BC), has been held as "the masterpiece of military strategy" and has provided significant orientation for military activities for over 2500 years. It illustrates a series of fundamental military rules and formulates systematic military theories by integrating the war experiences of the forefathers. Its influence has expanded from the ancient times to the modern times, from China to the world, from military operations to other areas of the society, attracting an increasing amount of attention across the world. To further publicize this military masterpiece and to herald the Beijing Olympics, the exhibition of "The Path to Victory—The Art of War and Fine Antiques of Ancient Chinese Military" will be jointly organized by the Military Museum of Chinese People's Revolution and Beijing Municipal Administration of Cultural Heritage.

　　The Exhibition in conjunction with the invaluable collections of twenty museums across the country, plainly reveals the quintessence of the ideas in The Art of War. These fine antiques are permeated with scientific and technological talents and carries the military history of ancient China,. They, as the military theories, are an important factor for the victory of war and represent the military cultural heritage shared by the mankind.

目　录

第一部分　兵学泰斗　横空出世 ………………………… 1

社会巨变的时代 …………………………………………… 2

    制度变革　技术进步 ………………………………… 2

    战争频繁　战法创新 ………………………………… 3

    百家争鸣　诸子涌现 ………………………………… 5

《孙子兵法》的问世 ……………………………………… 6

    将门出身　齐国成长 ………………………………… 6

    避走吴国　进献兵法 ………………………………… 9

    拜将统兵　战功卓著 ………………………………… 11

    图版 ………………………………………………… 13

第二部分　兵学圣典　博大精深 ………………………… 41

非危不战的慎战思想 ……………………………………… 42

    邯郸之战 …………………………………………… 42

知彼知己的战争认识思想 ………………………………… 46

    长勺之战 …………………………………………… 46

不战而屈人之兵的全胜思想 ……………………………… 47

    墨子救宋 …………………………………………… 47

    秦灭齐之战 ………………………………………… 49

致人而不致于人的主动思想 ……………………………… 50

    成皋之战 …………………………………………… 50

因敌变化而取胜的灵活作战思想 ………………………… 54

    官渡之战 …………………………………………… 54

    赤壁之战 …………………………………………… 56

兵者诡道的权变思想 ……………………………………… 57

　　参合陂之战 …………………………………………… 57

兵贵胜不贵久的速战思想 …………………………… 59

　　李愬袭蔡州之战 …………………………………… 59

未战而庙算的运筹思想 ……………………………… 61

　　北宋统一战争 ……………………………………… 61

　　桂陵之战 …………………………………………… 62

统兵用将的治军思想 ………………………………… 63

　　令文齐武的统兵之法 ……………………………… 63

　　必备五德的用将之道 ……………………………… 65

因粮于敌的后勤保障思想 …………………………… 67

　　清军收复新疆的战争 ……………………………… 67

图版 …………………………………………………… 69

第三部分　兵学哲理　魅力永存 …………………… 131

《孙子兵法》的传播和影响 ………………………… 132

　《孙子兵法》的传播 ……………………………… 132

　《孙子兵法》的当代影响 ………………………… 133

《孙子兵法》的现代评价 …………………………… 138

第四部分　古代军事专题 …………………………… 139

弓弩与远射 …………………………………………… 140

铠甲与防护 …………………………………………… 142

指南针的发明和使用 ………………………………… 144

火药与火器发明 ……………………………………… 146

军事通信 ……………………………………………… 148

图版 …………………………………………………… 151

先秦之言兵者六家，前孙子者，孙子不遗；后孙子者，不能遗孙子。

——（明）茅元仪

第一部分　兵学泰斗　横空出世
Part One Rising from Turmoil Master of Military Strategy

　　春秋时期（公元前770－前476年），中国开始由奴隶社会向封建社会过渡。王室衰微，诸侯争雄，列国兼并。社会的剧烈变动，使一批批思想巨人涌现、一个个传世学说创立。《孙子兵法》就是其中一颗璀璨的明星。

　　During the Spring and Autumn Period, China began to transform from slave society to feudal society. The royal family of Zhou Dynasty was on the wane, giving rise to belligerence among the hereditary nobles for over lordship and the annexation of smaller states. The tempestuous social unrest catalyzed a great number of great thinkers and countless new theories of far-reaching significance. The Art of War was one of the brilliant masterpieces.

制度变革　技术进步
Institutional Transformation　Technological Advances

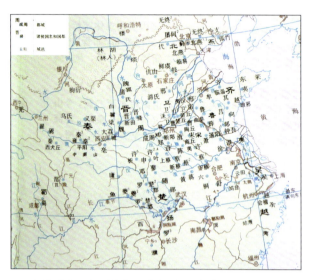

春秋时期，中国社会剧烈变动。诸侯争霸，列国兼并。周朝分封的"八百诸侯"，到春秋末只剩下40多个。图为春秋形势图。

春秋时期实行的"初税亩"、"用田赋"，事实上承认了土地个人私有。表明随着农业生产力不断提高，代表奴隶制度的井田制发生动摇，封建土地所有制开始萌芽。这是《左传》关于"初税亩"、"用田赋"的记载。

钢铁冶炼和制造技术逐步成熟。钢铁兵器开始使用。图为湖南长沙出土的春秋钢剑。

采矿、冶炼和铸造技术显著进步，制造工具和兵器的水平大幅度提高。图为1974年湖北大冶铜绿山发现的春秋铜矿井。

春秋炼铜用的木铲、竹火签和遗留的炉渣

春秋乳钉纹钟

战争频繁 战法创新
Continual Wars   Innovations in Military Tactics

春秋战争简表

春秋大国争霸战争	交战时间	交战国	交战地点	交战结果
郑灭胡之战	春秋初年	郑国 胡国	胡(今河南郾城南)	郑国袭灭胡国
北制之战	周桓王二年(公元前718年)	郑国 南燕	北制(今河南荥阳汜水镇)	郑军击败南燕军
郑抗北戎之战	周桓王六年(公元前714年)	郑国 北戎		郑军大败戎军
繻葛之战	周桓王十三年(公元前707年)	周王室 郑国	繻葛(今河南长葛东北)	郑军击败周联军
楚随战争	春秋初期	楚国 随国		随成为楚之附庸国
长勺之战	周庄王十三年(公元前684年)	鲁国 齐国	长勺(今山东曲阜北)	鲁军将齐军逐出鲁地
假途灭虢之战	春秋初期	晋国 虞国 虢国		晋灭虞、虢
韩之战	春秋初期	秦国 晋国	韩(今山西河津、万荣间)	秦晋两国盟于东城(今陕西大荔东)
泓水之战	春秋初期	宋国 楚国	泓水(今河南柘城北)	楚军击败宋军
商密之战	周襄王十八年(公元前634年)	秦国 鄀国	商密(今河南淅川西南)	秦军逼鄀南迁
城濮之战	周襄王二十一年(公元前632年)	晋国 楚国	城濮(今山东鄄城西南)	楚军兵败,晋文公取得中原霸权。
崤之战	周襄王二十六年(公元前627年)	晋国 秦国	崤山(今河南陕县东南)	秦军全部被歼
楚灭庸之战	周匡王二年(公元前611年)	楚国 庸国		楚灭庸国
邲之战	周定王十年(公元前597年)	晋国 楚国	邲(今河南荥阳东北)	晋国丧失长达数十年的霸主地位,楚国夺得中原霸权
鞍之战	周定王十八年(公元前589年)	晋国 齐国	鞍(今济南西北)	晋国战胜齐国
鄢陵之战	周简王十一年(公元前575年)	晋国 楚国	鄢陵(今河南鄢陵西北)	晋国战胜楚国
庸浦之战	周灵王十三年(公元前560年)	楚国 吴国	庸浦(今安徽无为南长江北)	楚军击败吴军
皋舟之战	周灵王十三年(公元前559年)	吴国 楚国	皋舟(约在今安徽巢湖以北一带)	吴军大败楚军
平阴之战	周灵王十七年(公元前555年)	以晋为首的诸侯联军 齐国	平阴(今山东平阴东北)	齐军遭受打击
楚灭舒鸠之战	周灵王二十四年(公元前548年)	楚国 吴国	舒鸠(今安徽舒城东南)	楚军击败吴军,楚灭舒鸠。
长岸之战	周景王二十年(公元前525年)	吴国 楚国	长岸(今安徽当涂西南)	吴军大败楚军
鸡父之战	周敬王元年(公元前519年)	吴国 楚联军	鸡父(今河南固始东南)	吴军大败楚联军
柏举之战	周敬王十四年(公元前506年)	吴国 楚国	柏举(今湖北麻城东北)	吴军击败楚军
槜李之战	周敬王二十四年(公元前496年)	吴国 越国	槜李(今浙江嘉兴、桐乡间)	越军击败吴军
铁之战	周敬王二十七年(公元前493年)	晋国 郑国	铁(今河南濮阳西北)	晋军击败郑军
艾陵之战	周敬王三十六年(公元前484年)	吴国 齐国	艾陵(今山东莱芜东北)	吴军击败齐军
姑苏之战	周敬王三十八年(公元前482年)	越国 吴国	吴(今江苏苏州)	越军袭破吴国都城吴
笠泽之战	周敬王四十二年(公元前478年)	越国 吴国	笠泽(今江苏苏州南)	越军大破吴军

春秋盟书又称"载书",是卿大夫之间为了在政治利益上相互约束而订立的盟誓载词。一式两份,一份藏于盟府,一份埋于地下或沉入河中,以取信于鬼神。该盟书年代为公元前497年,盟主是韩氏宗主。(河南省文物考古研究所提供)

春秋战车遗迹

春秋战术战法发展简表

年 代	实施国	指挥者	战术、战法	运用战例	效果
公元前718年	郑	庄公	迂回	郑卫北制之战	郑军胜
公元前714年	郑	公子突	伏击	郑抗北戎之战	郑军胜
公元前712年	郑	颍考叔	强攻登城	郑灭许之战	郑军胜
公元前707年	郑	子元	"鱼丽之阵",两翼攻击	周郑繻葛之战	郑军胜
公元前684年	鲁	曹刿	后发制人	齐鲁长勺之战	鲁军胜
公元前632年	晋	文公、先轸	诈退诱敌、侧击、夹击	晋楚城濮之战	晋军胜
公元前615年	晋	臾骈	野战筑垒	秦晋河曲之战	晋军胜
公元前584年	吴	不详	连续作战	吴楚州来之战	吴军胜
公元前570年	吴	不详	"要(腰)击"	吴楚衡山之战	吴军胜
公元前549年	楚	康王	"舟师"讨伐	楚攻吴	楚军无功而还
公元前541年	晋	魏舒	"毁车为行"	晋狄大原之战	晋军胜
公元前525年	吴	公子光	潜水手袭扰	吴楚长岸之战	吴军胜
公元前506年	楚	针尹固	"燧(火)象"攻击	吴楚柏举之战	楚军击退追兵
公元前504年	吴、楚	太子终、潘子臣	"舟师"水战	吴楚水陆之战	吴军胜
公元前485年	吴	徐承	"舟师"渡海作战	吴舟师攻齐之战	齐军胜
公元前478年	越	勾践(王)	两翼佯攻、中间突破	吴越笠泽之战	越军胜

青铜器上的战车纹饰

战车是春秋时期陆战的主要装备。每车载甲士三名，按左、中、右排列。左方甲士持弓，是一车之长；右方甲士执戈；居中甲士驾驭战车。车上一般还备有其他兵器，供甲士选用。以战车为中心，配以若干徒兵及后勤车辆和徒役，组成车战的基本单位——乘。

春秋矛状车軎　安装在车轴两端，具有防护和杀伤功能。（湖北省博物馆提供）

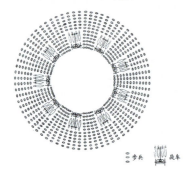

阵，是作战队形。实战中因敌情、地形、天候等不同而发生变化。阵形多样，但基本阵形为方阵（进攻队形）、圆阵（防守队形）两种。

春秋车軎、车辖

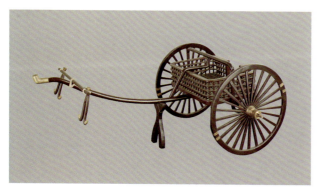

春秋战车模型

西周蟠虺纹车輨（河南博物院提供）

4

春秋铜戈

春秋铜矛

春秋铜剑

百家争鸣 诸子涌现

The Contention of One Hundred Schools of Thought
The Springing up of Master Thinkers

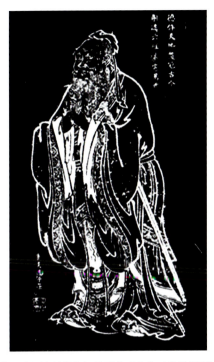

　　春秋时期，在思想领域出现了"百家争鸣"的活跃局面。一批思想家应时而生，形成了多种学派。

　　孔子(公元前551—前479年)名丘，字仲尼，鲁国人，春秋后期伟大的思想家、教育家，儒家学派创始人。

　　老子(春秋末)，又称老聃,姓李，名耳，字聃，据传为楚国苦县(今河南鹿邑)人。春秋末年思想家、道家学派创始人。

管子(?—公元前645年),名夷吾,又名敬仲、字仲,生于颍上(颍水之滨),春秋初期齐国政治家、军事家。

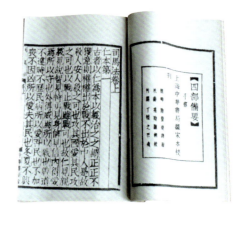

《司马法》是反映春秋及其以前军事理论的名著。

墨子(春秋末战国初),姓墨,名翟,鲁国人,春秋战国之际思想家、政治家,墨家学派创始人。

《论语》、《老子》《墨子》、《管子》等著作

《孙子兵法》的问世
Advent of The Art of War

将门出身　齐国成长
Born in An Army General's Family　　Growth in the State of Qi

军事理论家。其曾祖父、祖父都是善于带兵作战的将领。孙武赴吴国进献兵法,任将军,击败楚、越,威服齐、晋,立下功勋。所著《孙子兵法》对后世有巨大而深远的影响。

孙子,名武,字长卿,春秋末期齐国人,中国古代著名

《史记》关于孙武事迹的记载

《新唐书》关于孙武祖父田书伐莒及赐为孙姓的记载。

《左传》关于孙武祖父田书伐莒的记载。

姜太公，又称吕望，字子牙，商周之际军事家。辅佐周武王灭商，建立西周王朝，后封于齐（今山东境）。史称兵法谋略始祖。

战车的数量是诸侯国军力强弱的标志.齐国当时称为"千乘之国"。这是位于山东临淄的春秋齐国车马坑。

齐桓公（？—公元前643年），姜姓，名小白。春秋初期齐国国君。任用贤臣，推行经济、政治、军事改革，成为春秋时期第一位霸主。 作者 申晓轶

司马穰苴，本姓田，春秋后期齐国大夫，军事家。曾率兵击退晋、燕大军。治军严整，深通兵法。其军事言论被收入《司马法》一书。

春秋战国齐国刀币(山东省博物馆提供)

临淄（今属山东淄博），春秋战国时期齐国都城，当时中国东部经济、文化中心。图为齐国都城遗址。

春秋齐国铜戈

春秋齐国铜剑

苏州穹隆山孙武隐居纪念地

避走吴国　进献兵法
Depart to the State of Wu　Presentation of the Book of
Military Strategy

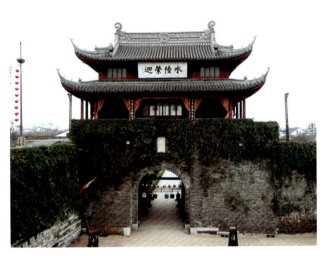

春秋末年，孙武为躲避齐国内乱投奔吴国，在吴国大夫伍子胥的推荐下，将《兵法》十三篇进献吴王阖闾。

吴国都城，又称阖闾城，位于今江苏苏州。图为明清时期苏州城遗址。

伍子胥（？—公元前484年），名员，春秋末期吴国大夫，军事家。他胸怀大略，远见卓识，和孙武一道辅佐吴王治军经邦，使吴国迅速强盛。

春秋高子戈（山东省博物馆提供）

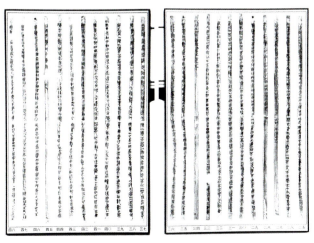

伍子胥的兵法著作《盖庐》

山东临沂银雀山汉墓竹简发掘现场

不貴無義今吾貪生棄行非義也夫人有三惡以立於世吾何面目以視天下之士言訖遂投身於江未絶從者出之要離曰吾寧能不死乎從者曰君且勿死以俟爵禄要離乃自斷手足伏劍而死 三年吳將欲伐楚王問子胥白喜相謂曰吾等為王興師畫其策謀有利於國而子胥白喜故伐楚奈何有於二子何如子胥白喜對曰臣願用命吳王内計二子

皆怨楚深恐以兵往破滅而已登臺向南風而嘯有頃而嘆羣臣莫知吳意者子胥知王之不足乃薦孫子於王孫子者名武吳人也善為兵法辟隱深居世人莫知其能胥乃明知鑒辨知孫子可以折衝銷敵乃一旦與吳王論兵七薦孫子吳王曰子胥託言進士欲以自納而名孫子問曰兵法寧可以小試耶孫子曰可可以小試於後宮之女王曰諾孫子曰得大王寵姬二人以為

《吴越春秋》关于孙武与吴王论兵的记载

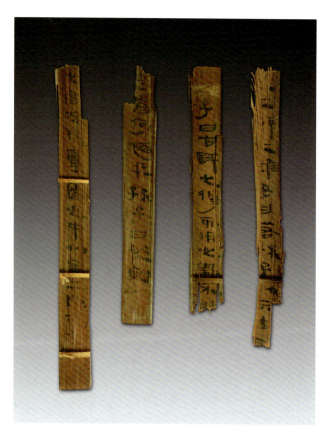

《孙子兵法》竹简　1972年山东临沂银雀山汉墓出土。同时还出土了《孙膑兵法》竹简。解决了学术界长期争论的问题，证明孙武和孙膑各有其人，各有其书。（山东省博物馆提供）

吴王阖闾极为看重孙武的兵法，以180名宫女予孙武教战试兵。孙武将宫女分为两队，以吴王的两位宠姬分任队长。宫女不听号令，嬉笑不止。孙武斩宠姬以严军令，充分显示了他的胆识和治军才能。

拜将统兵　战功卓著

Appointed as General, in command of the Army
Conspicuous Battle Achievements

吴宫教战后，吴王拜孙武为将。公元前506年，伍子胥、孙武等率领吴军进攻楚国，在柏举(今湖北麻城东北)击败楚军主力,进而攻破楚都郢。

勾践（？—公元前465年），春秋末期越国国君。公元前494年兵败夫椒后，在文种、范蠡辅佐下，"卧薪尝胆"，励精图治，使国家由弱到强，最终灭亡吴国。　作者　申晓轶

柏举之战战场遗址(今湖北麻城东北)

夫差（？—公元前473年），春秋末期吴国国君。
作者　陈钰铭

公元前494年，越王勾践率军攻吴。吴王夫差和伍子胥、孙武指挥吴军在夫椒（今江苏太湖洞庭山）大败越军。越王勾践向吴求和。图为夫椒之战战场遗址。

春秋吴国大翼战船

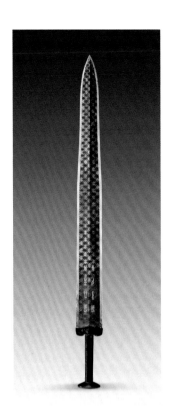

越王勾践剑，剑身有八个鸟篆铭文"越王鸠浅(勾践)自乍(作)用劎(剑)"。（湖北省博物馆提供）

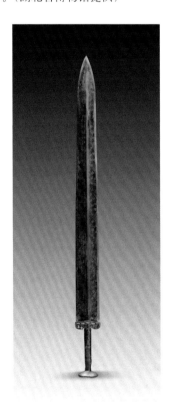

春秋战国时期吴越青铜剑在合金配比、铸造淬炼、表面处理、形制设计等方面都达到很高水平。几千年后出土时，仍然光亮如新、锋利无比，世所罕见。这是战国越王州句剑。（浙江省博物馆提供）

战国越王丌北古剑（安庆市博物馆提供）

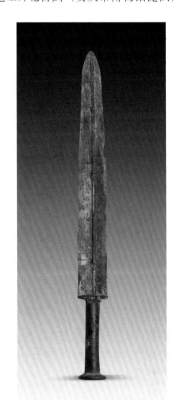

春秋战国吴太子姑发剑（安徽省博物馆提供）

12

春秋乳钉纹钟　　上直径29厘米　　下直径39厘米　　高45厘米
Bronze Bell with repousse pattern of the Spring and Autumn Period
Diameter, 29 cm (top); 39 cm (bottom); height, 45 cm

春秋矛状车軎　曽侯乙墓出土　湖北省博物馆提供
Spear-shaped Hub Cap of the Spring and Autumn Period
Excavated from Zenghouyi Tomb, provided by Hubei Provincial Museum

春秋车軎、车辖　长 11.5 厘米　宽 11 厘米
Hub Cap and Linchpin of the Spring and Autumn Period
Length, 11.5 cm; width, 11 cm

西周蟠虺纹车辖　长6.3厘米　直径8.6厘米　1990年河南平顶山应国墓地出土　河南博物院提供
Bronze Axle-head Cover with curved spousse of the Western Zhou Dynasty
Length, 6.3 cm; width, 8.6 cm
Excavated from graveyard of Ying State, Pingding Hill, Henan Province, 1990, provided by Henan Provincial
 Museum

春秋铜戈　（上）长 21.1 厘米　宽 11 厘米　（下）长 23 厘米　宽 12 厘米
Bronze Daggers of the Spring and Autumn Period
Length, 21.1 cm; width, 11 cm (top)
Length, 23 cm; width, 12 cm (bottom)

春秋铜矛 （左）长14厘米 宽2厘米 （中）长20厘米 宽4厘米 （右）长25厘米 宽4厘米
Bronze Spears of the Spring and Autumn Period
Length, 14 cm; width, 2 cm (left)
Length, 20 cm; width, 4 cm (middle)
Length, 25 cm; width, 4 cm (right)

春秋盟书　河南省文物考古研究所提供
The Covenant of the Spring and Autumn Period
Provided by the Henan Research Institute for Cultural Heritage and Archaeology

春秋盟书　河南省文物考古研究所提供
The Covenant of the Spring and Autumn Period
Provided by the Henan Research Institute for Cultural Heritage and Archaeology

春秋盟书　河南省文物考古研究所提供
The Covenant of the Spring and Autumn Period
Provided by the Henan Research Institute for Cultural Heritage and Archaeology

春秋齐国铜戈　长 20.5 厘米　宽 11 厘米
Bronze Dagger of the State of Qi of the Spring and Autumn Period
Length, 20.5 cm; width, 11 cm

春秋铜剑　长 47.5 厘米　宽 4.3 厘米
Bronze Sword of the Spring and Autumn Period
Length, 47.5 cm; width, 4.3 cm

春秋齐国铜剑　长 43.5 厘米　宽 3.5 厘米
Bronze Sword of the State of Qi of the Spring and Autumn Period
Length, 43.5 cm; width, 3.5 cm

春秋战国齐国刀币　山东省博物馆提供
Knife-shaped Coins Issued by the State of Qi of the Spring and Autumn Period
Provided by Shandong Provincial Museum

春秋战国齐国刀币　山东省博物馆提供
Knife-shaped Coins Issued by the State of Qi of the Spring and Autumn Period
Provided by Shandong Provincial Museum

春秋战国齐国刀币　山东省博物馆提供
Knife-shaped Coins Issued by the State of Qi of the Spring and Autumn Period
Provided by Shandong Provincial Museum

西汉《孙子兵法》竹简　山东省博物馆提供
The Bamboo Slips of the Art of War of Western Han Dynasty
Provided by Shandong Provincial Museum

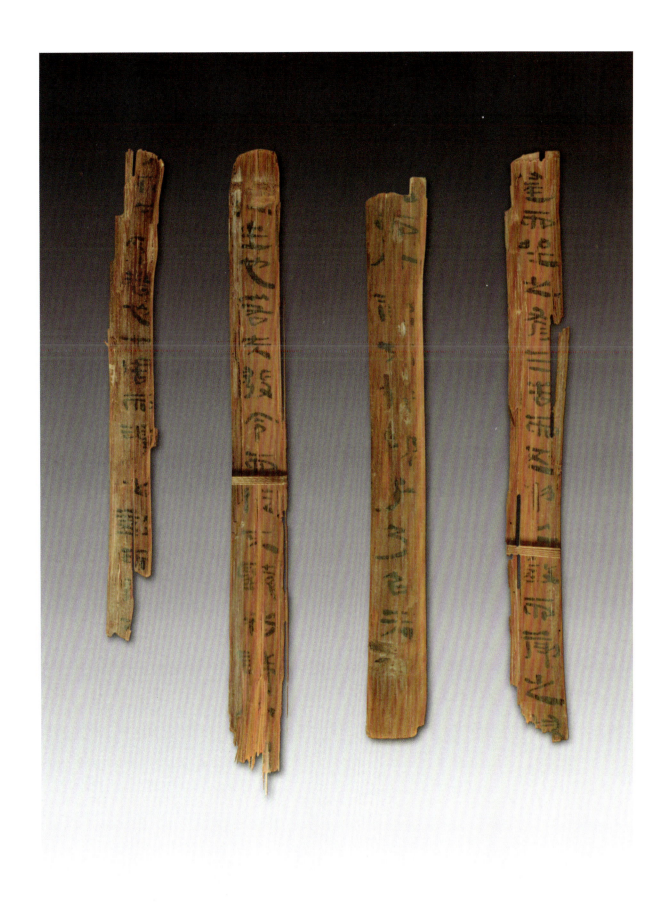

西汉《孙子兵法》竹简　山东省博物馆提供
The Bamboo Slips of the Art of War of Western Han Dynasty
Provided by Shandong Provincial Museum

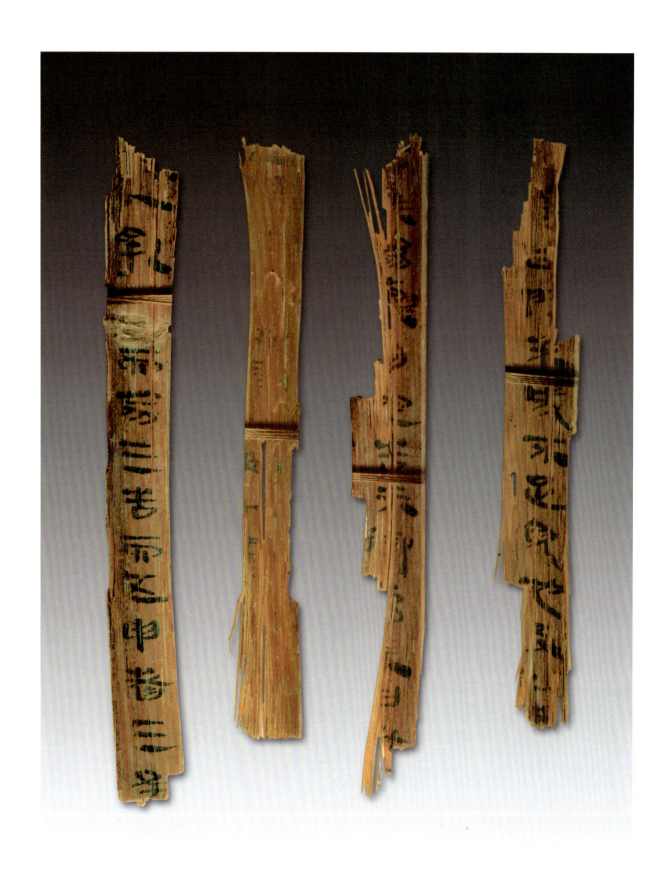

西汉《孙子兵法》竹简　山东省博物馆提供
The Bamboo Slips of the Art of War of Western Han Dynasty
Provided by Shandong Provincial Museum

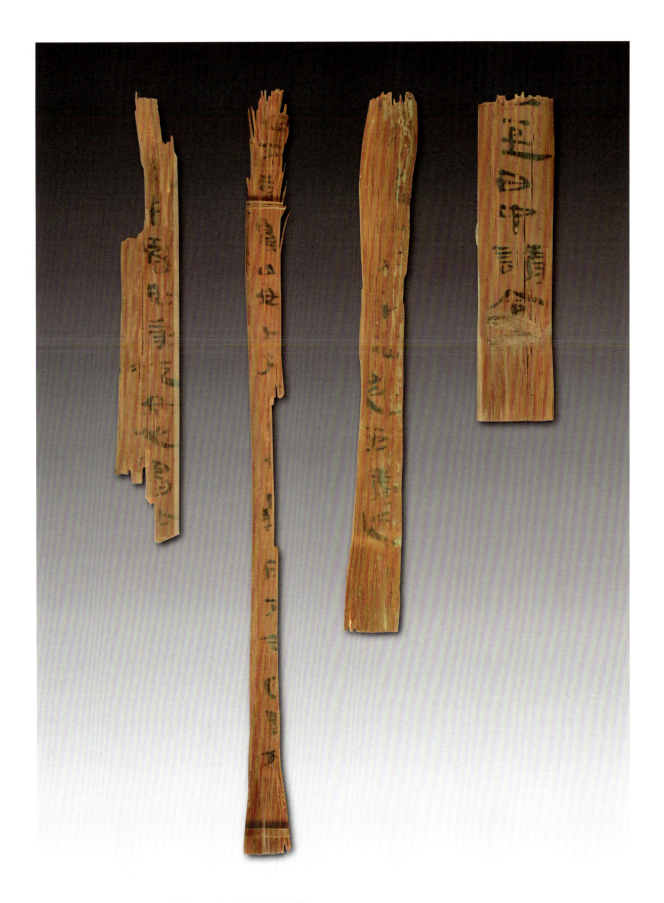

西汉《孙子兵法》竹简　山东省博物馆提供
The Bamboo Slips of the Art of War of Western Han Dynasty
Provided by Shandong Provincial Museum

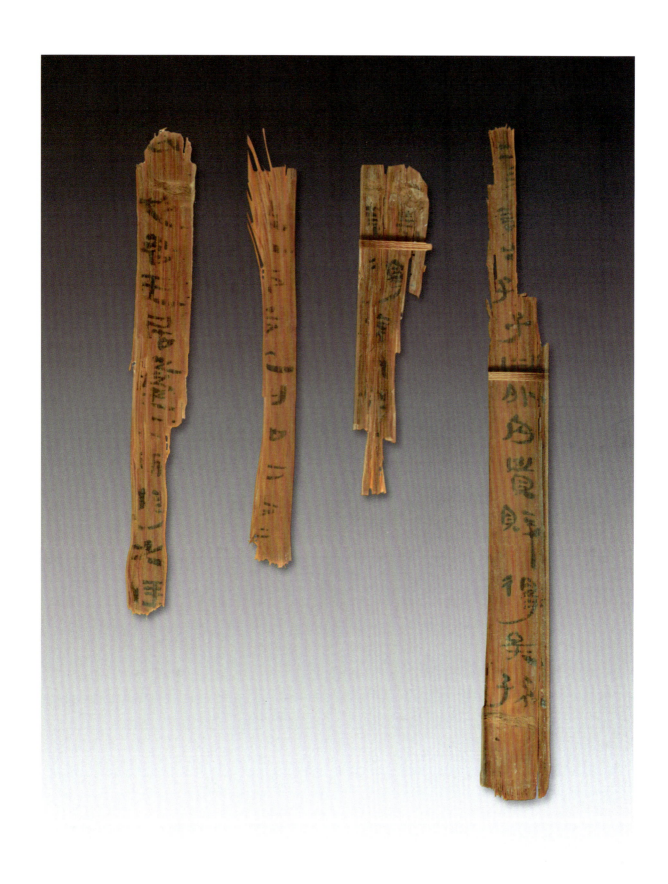

西汉《孙子兵法》竹简　山东省博物馆提供
The Bamboo Slips of the Art of War of Western Han Dynasty
Provided by Shandong Provincial Museum

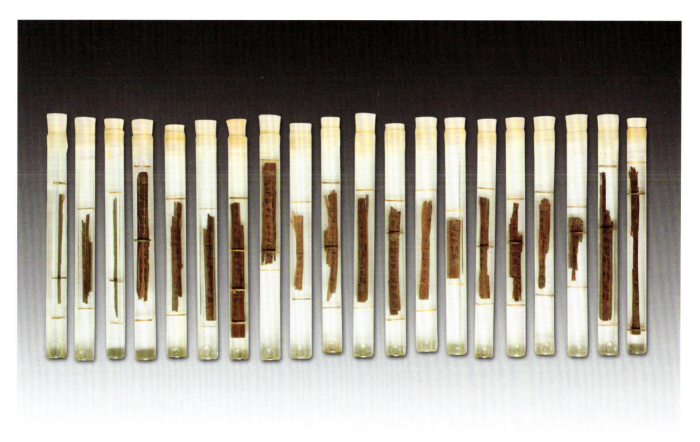

　　《孙子兵法》竹简 1972 年山东临沂银雀山汉墓出土。同时还出土了《孙膑兵法》竹简。解决了学术界长期争论的问题，证明孙武和孙膑各有其人，各有其书。山东省博物馆提供。

　　The Bamboo Slips of the Art of War, excavated from the Tomb of Han Dynasty in Yinque Hill, Linyi, Shandong Province in 1972. The bamboo slips of Sun Bin Military Tactics were also discovered there. The discovery stands as proof that Sun Tzu and Sun Bin are two different authors of two different books, thus putting an end to a long-disputed question in the academic circle. provided by Shandong Provincial Museum

春秋高子戈　通长29厘米　宽2.7厘米　山东临淄出土　山东省博物馆提供
The Gaozi Dagger of the Spring and Autumn Period
Length, 29 cm; width, 2.7 cm
Excavated from Linzi，Shandong Province, provided by Shandong Provincial Museum

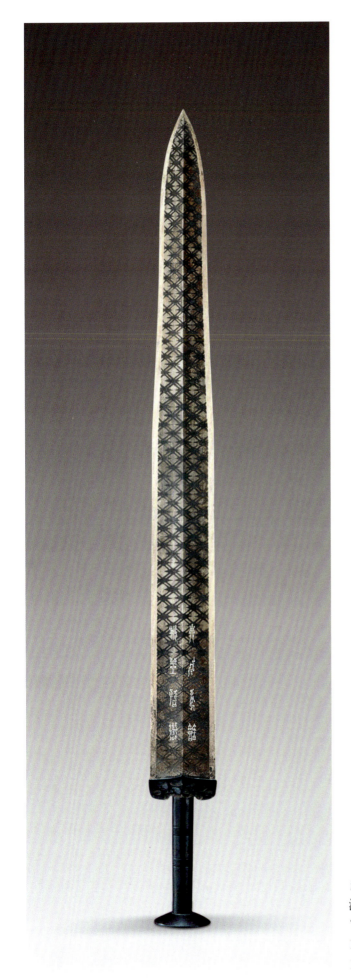

越王勾践剑局部
Part of the Sword of Gou Jian

越王勾践剑　长55.6厘米　剑格宽5厘米
湖北省博物馆提供
The Sword of Gou Jian, the King of Yue
Length, 55.6 cm; width, 5 cm
Provided by Hubei Provincial Museum

战国越王州句剑　长57厘米　浙江省博物馆提供
The Sword of Zhou Gou, the King of Yue of the Period of Warring State
Length, 57 cm
Provided by Zhejiang Provincial Museum

战国越王丌北古剑　长64厘米　剑格宽4.5厘米　安庆市博物馆提供
The Sword of Qi Beigu, the King of Yue of the Period of Warring State
Length, 64 cm; width, 4.5 cm
Provided by Anqing Municipal Museum

春秋吴太子姑发剑　安徽省博物馆提供
The Sword of Gufa, the Prince of the State of Wu, the Spring and Autumn Period
Provided by Anhui Provincial Museum

第二部分 兵学圣典 博大精深
Part Two Masterpiece of Military Strategy, Extensive and Profound

　　《孙子兵法》十三篇为：计、作战、谋攻、形、势、虚实、军争、九变、行军、地形、九地、火攻、用间，涵盖了战争观、战略、战术、后勤保障、治军用将等各个方面，体系完备，博大精深，被公认为世界上现存最早、体系完备的军事理论著作。

　　The Art of war is composed of 13 chapters — Laying Plans, Waging War, Attack by Stratagem, Disposition of Military Strength, Use of Energy, Weaknesses and Strengths, Manoeuvring, Variation of Tactics, On the March, Terrain, the Nine Varieties of Ground, Attack by Fire and Use of Spies. Boasting self-contained organization, extensiveness and profoundness, it covers an array of aspects such as the view of war, military strategy, military tactics, logistics, the commanding of the army and the arrangement of generals etc. It is recognized as the earliest literature in the world on military theory with a logical theoretical system.

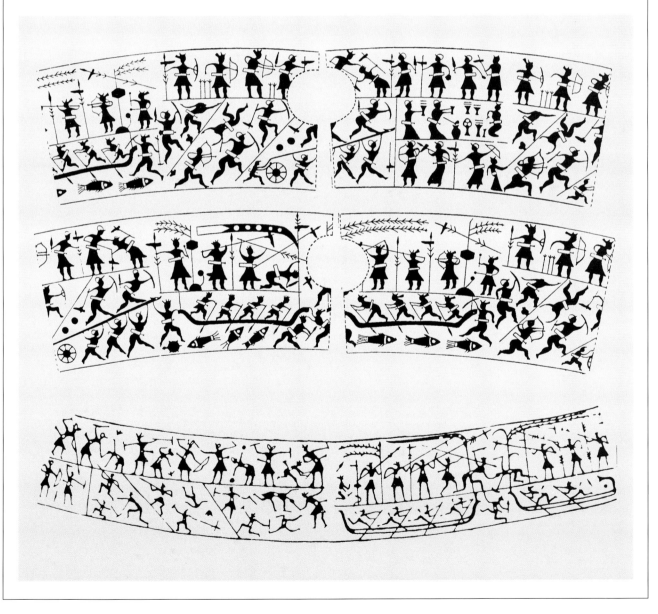

"兵者，国之大事，死生之地，存亡之道，不可不察也。"（计篇）

War is a matter of vital importance to the state; a matter of life and death, the road either to survival or to ruin. Hence, it is imperative that it be thoroughly studied.

"非利不动，非得不用，非危不战。主不可以怒而兴师，将不可以愠而致战。"（火攻篇）

If not in the interests of the state, do not act. If you are not sure of success, do not use troops. If you are not in danger, do not fight a battle. A sovereign should not launch a war simply out of anger, nor should a general fight a war simply out of resentment.

邯郸之战
The Battle of Handan

公元前258年，秦昭王为索取赵国6城，贸然出兵进攻赵都邯郸，屡攻不下。秦昭王改换白起指挥。白起认为赵国仍有一定实力，又有魏、楚两国援军，攻赵条件不成熟，拒绝赴命，并力劝罢兵。秦昭王一意孤行，继续增兵，被赵、魏、楚联军击败。

白起(?～公元前257)，郿(今陕西眉县东)人，战国时期秦国军事家。秦昭王时主要将领，率军攻城掠地，消灭敌国大量兵力，奠定了秦统一六国的基础。

赵王城遗址，位于河北邯郸西南

赵邯郸城夯土遗迹

赵长城遗址，位于河南沁阳境。

战国铁剑

战国郾王喜矛(河北省文物研究所提供)

战国铁矛头

战国左行议率戈(河北省文物研究所提供)

战国两色剑

秦弩机

秦铜镞

战国二戈戟(湖北省博物馆提供)

战国铜矛(湖北省博物馆提供)

战国三戈戟　三件戈安装在同一个柄上，有很强的杀伤力。(湖北省博物馆提供)

战国铜戈(湖北省博物馆提供)

战国铜殳(湖北省博物馆提供)

战国铜箭镞(湖北省博物馆提供)

战国三十三年郑令铍(河南博物院提供)

战国铜戈(河南省文物考古研究所提供)

战国素面薄格剑(河南博物院提供)

战国兵避太岁戈(荆州博物馆提供)

战国铜矛(河南省文物考古研究所提供)

"知彼知已，百战不殆。"（谋攻篇）

Know the enemy and know yourself, and you can fight a hundred battles with no danger of defeat.

"知彼知已，胜乃不殆；知天知地，胜乃可全。"（地形篇）

Know the enemy and know yourself, and your victory will never be endangered; know the weather and know the ground, and your victory will then be complete.

长勺之战
The Battle of Changshao

公元前684年，齐国大举进犯鲁国，鲁庄公准备出战。国人曹刿问他有什么取胜把握，从对鲁庄公治国政策的分析中判断此战能得到人民支持，于是要求随鲁庄公指挥作战。齐、鲁两军对阵于长勺。曹刿深知，军队制胜靠"气"，强弱可以转化，建议庄公在齐军三次击鼓已是兵疲意沮后发起进攻，"一鼓作气"战胜强敌。察看齐军"辙乱"、"旗靡"，确实溃败时，下令追击，将齐军逐出鲁境。

① ②

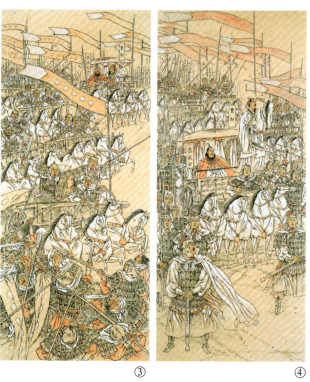

③ ④

长勺之战　①曹刿论战、②待敌衰竭、③一鼓作气、④令逐齐师　作者 柴山林、朱振芳

《左传》关于长勺之战的记载

长勺之战战场遗址，位于山东莱芜北。

东汉曹子劫桓画像石（拓片）　公元前681年，曹刿劫持齐桓公，为鲁国索回被齐国侵占的土地。

不战而屈人之兵的全胜思想
The Thinking of Achieving Complete Victory: To subdue the enemy without fighting

"是故百战百胜，非善之善者也；不战而屈人之兵，善之善者也。"（谋攻篇）

Hence to win one hundred victories in one hundred battles is not the acme of skill. To subdue the enemy without fighting is the supreme excellence.

"全国为上，破国次之；全军为上，破军次之；全旅为上，破旅次之；全卒为上，破卒次之；全伍为上，破伍次之。"（谋攻篇）

Generally in war the best thing of all is to take the enemy's state whole and intact, to ruin it is inferior to this. To capture the enemy's army entire is better than to destroy it; to take intact a battalion, a company or a five-man squad is better that to destroy them.

墨子救宋
Mozi Came to Rescue the State of Song

战国时期，墨子得知楚王令公输般（鲁班）制造云梯，准备攻打弱小的宋国，遂派弟子到宋国帮助防守，并亲自赶到楚国劝阻。墨子解下腰带比作城墙，与公输般推演攻守战法。公输般设制九种攻城方法，被墨子一一破解。楚王只得放弃攻宋的打算。

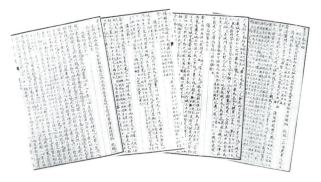

《墨子·公输》记载了墨子救宋的事迹。

《墨子·备城门》诸篇记载了各种守城战法。

墨子救宋　作者　邓超华

47

云梯

抛石机

撞车

辒辒车

塞门刀车

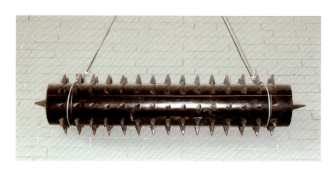

木擂

砖擂

泥擂

秦灭齐之战
The Battle where the State of Qin Destroyed the State of Qi

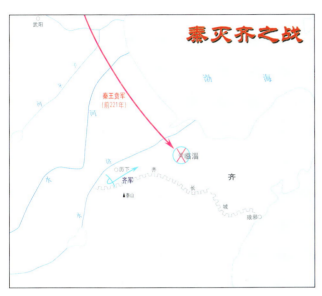

　　秦在统一六国战争中，一面攻打韩、赵、魏、楚、燕五国，一面向齐国派出间谍，收买重臣，通过他们对齐王威吓利诱，使齐国疏远与他国的关系，放松对秦国的戒备。公元前221年，秦将王贲率军避开齐军正面防御，由齐国北部突入，包围王城，迫使齐王建不战而降。

　　秦兵马俑坑，位于陕西临潼。坑中数千兵马俑，体现了秦国的强大军事实力。

齐长城遗址，位于山东蓬莱境。

秦长城遗址，位于内蒙古固阳西北阿塔山。

相邦七年铜戟

49

秦铜剑

战国双钺形铜戈(云南省博物馆提供)

战国铜带钩

战国中山侯钺(河北省博物馆提供)

致人而不致于人的主动思想
The Thinking of Taking Initiatives: To bring the enemy to the field of battle and not to be brought there by him

"故善战者，致人而不致于人。"（虚实篇）

One skilled in war brings the enemy to the field of battle and is not brought there by him.

"敢问：敌众整而将来，待之若何？曰：先夺其所爱，则听矣。"（九地篇）

Should one ask: "How do I cope with a well-ordered enemy host about to attack me?" I reply: "Seize something he cherishes and he will conform to your desires."

成皋之战
The Battle of Chenggao

攻城掠地，迫使项羽多次回救，疲于奔命，由主动变为被动。汉军最终夺取成皋，为灭楚兴汉奠定了坚实的基础。

汉霸二王城遗址，位于河南荥阳广武山。

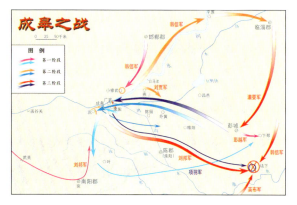

公元前205年，刘邦与项羽争夺战略要地成皋（今河南荥阳西）。在正面交锋的同时，刘邦命韩信等人在项羽侧后方

刘邦(公元前247~前195年)，沛县(今属江苏)人。汉朝开国皇帝，著名政治家。

项羽(公元前232～前202年)名籍，下相(今江苏宿迁西)人。秦末反秦义军重要领袖、名将。史称"西楚霸王"。

汉代铁钻(湖北省考古研究所提供)

韩信(?～公元前196年)淮阴(今江苏淮阴西南)人，秦末汉初著名军事家。

汉代铁刀

汉代铜凿(湖北省考古研究所提供)

汉代铁剑

汉代铁戟

建武三十二年铜弩机(河北省文物研究所提供)

汉代铜弩机

汉代陶带扣范(河南博物院提供)

汉代铜箭镞

东汉手搏画像砖(南阳市文物考古研究所提供)

西汉彩绘带冠红衣长甲扛械俑(咸阳博物馆提供)(左)
西汉步兵俑（右）

西汉彩绘骑马俑(咸阳博物馆提供)

西汉驻军图　中国迄今发现最早的军用地图。湖南长沙马王堆出土(湖南省博物馆提供)。长98、宽78厘米。上南下北,于今地图相反。标绘区域位于今湖南南部宁远九嶷山与南岭之间,绘有山脉、河流、居民点等,着重标出9支部队的住地、防区、军事设施和行动路线。

西汉战争贮贝器(云南省博物馆提供)

东汉胡汉战争画像砖(河南博物院提供)

西汉战争贮贝器器盖反映滇人和昆明人之间的战争。贝是当时的一种货币。

因敌变化而取胜的灵活作战思想
The Thinking of Being Flexible in War：Defeating the enemy with timely changes

"故兵无常势，水无常形。能因敌变化而取胜者，谓之神。"（虚实篇）

There are neither fixed postures nor constant tactics in warfare. He who can modify his tactics in accordance with the enemy situation and thereby succeeds in winning may be said to be divine.

"夫兵形象水，水之形避高而趋下，兵之形避实而击虚。"（虚实篇）

Now, the laws of military operations are like water. The tendency of water is to flow from heights to lowlands. The law of successful operations is to avoid the enemy's strength and strike his weakness.

官渡之战
The Battle of Guandu

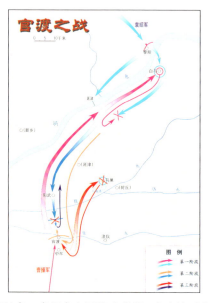

公元200年，袁绍率大军进攻曹操，在官渡（今河南中牟东北）地区展开决战。曹操抓住袁绍自恃粮足兵多、执意正面作战的特点，亲率精兵奇袭袁军屯粮处乌巢，火烧全部粮草，致使袁军军心动摇，曹军乘势发动正面进攻，大败袁军，奠定了统一北方的基础。

官渡之战遗址，位于河南中牟东北。

曹操（155～220年），字孟德，沛国谯（今安徽亳州）人。汉末著名军事家、政治家和文学家，史称魏武帝，精通《孙子兵法》，注重谋略，灵活作战，长于用将，治军严整，著有《孙子略解》。

魏晋执骑兵图（画像砖）　1972年甘肃嘉峪关魏晋墓出土

魏晋墓步兵出行图（画像砖）　1972年甘肃嘉峪关魏晋墓出土

《曹操集》

吾观兵书战策多矣，孙武所著深矣！……审计重举明画深图，不可相诬。

——曹操

三国铜矛、墩

三国撞车头

三国部曲将印

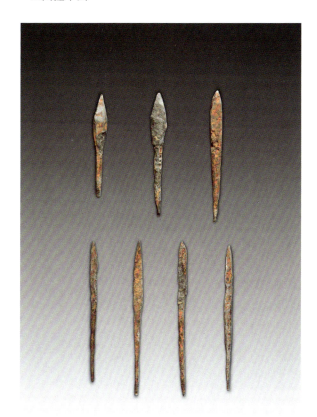

三国铁镞

三国别部司马

赤壁之战
The Battle of Chibi

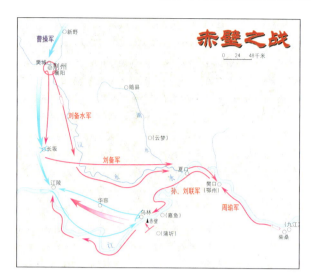

公元 208 年，曹操率大军进攻孙权、刘备联军，双方在长江赤壁(今湖北赤壁市西北)一带隔江对峙。孙刘联军针对曹军后方不安、远道劳师、水土不服、不习水战等弱点，利用曹军战船连锁之机，巧用火攻，大败曹军，从此奠定了三国鼎立格局。

赤壁之战遗址，位于湖北赤壁。

周瑜（公元 175～210 年），字公瑾，庐江舒县(今安徽庐江西南)人。三国时期军事家。公元 208 年，在赤壁之战中指挥孙刘联军大败曹军。

诸葛亮(公元 181～234 年)，字孔明，琅邪郡阳都县(今山东沂南南)人。三国时期著名政治家、军事家。蜀国丞相。

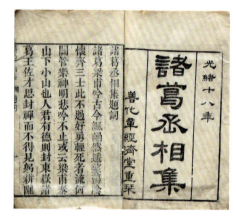

《诸葛丞相集》

赤壁之战　作者 郑洪流

三国蒙冲战船模型

三国木牛车模型

三国铜蒺藜

孙武所以能制胜于天下者，用法明也。

——诸葛亮

三国铁镞范(河南博物院提供)

兵者诡道的权变思想
The Thinking of Contingency Approach: All warfare is based on deception

"兵者，诡道也。"（计篇）

All warfare is based on deception.

"故兵以诈立，以利动，以分合为变者也。"（军争篇）

Now, war is based on deception. Move when it is advantageous and change tactics by dispersal and concentration of your troops.

参合陂之战
The Battle of Canhebei

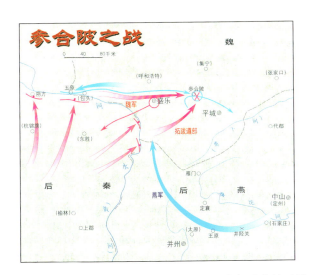

公元395年，后燕大举进攻北魏。北魏主拓跋圭针对后

燕恃强轻敌，采取示弱远避、待疲而击的方针，将主力撤回黄河南岸，与后燕军隔黄河对峙，并切断后燕前后方联系，假传后燕主慕容垂已死的消息，动摇敌方军心。然后乘燕军回撤，昼夜兼程、隐蔽追击，在参合陂(今内蒙古凉城东北)大败后燕军。此后北魏势力进入中原。

北魏南都平城遗址，位于山西大同东北。

西晋屯营图(画像砖) 1972年甘肃嘉峪关魏晋墓出土

西魏作战图(壁画)甘肃敦煌第285窟

南朝马具装图(画像砖) 1958年河南邓州出土

北朝高领长甲侍卫俑（左上）；北朝套衣风帽侍卫俑
（右上）；北朝负箭箙小冠俑（左下）；北朝负箭箙俑（右下）

西晋骑俑

北朝武士俑

西晋持盾武士俑

"故兵贵胜，不贵久。"（作战篇）

Hence, what is valued in war is a quick victory, not prolonged operations.

"兵之情主速，乘人之不及，由不虞之道，攻其所不戒也。"（九地篇）

Speed is the essence of war. Take advantage of the enemy's unpreparedness, make your way by unexpected routes, and attack him where he has taken no precautions.

李愬袭蔡州之战
The Battle in which Li Shuo Attacked Caizhou

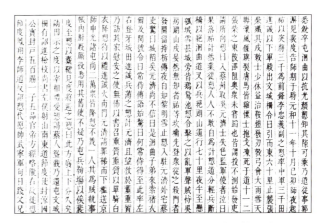

《新唐书·李晟传》关于李愬雪夜袭蔡州的记载

公元817年，唐朝随邓节度使李愬奉命平息吴元济叛乱，利用雪夜掩护，倍道兼程，出其不意袭破蔡州（治今河南汝南），吴元济被迫投降。

唐代仪仗壁画　陕西乾县懿德太子墓出土

李愬雪夜袭蔡州　作者 邓超华

隋代虎符

唐代彩绘红陶虎头帽武士俑(昭陵博物馆提供)

隋代箭镞

唐代粉彩金甲武士俑

唐代彩绘贴金甲马骑兵俑(陕西历史博物馆提供)

唐代三彩骑射俑

"夫未战而庙算胜者，得算多也。未战而庙算不胜者，得算少也。多算胜，少算不胜，而况于无算乎？吾以此观之，胜负见矣。"（计篇）

Now, the commander who gets many scores during the calculations in the temple before the war will have more likelihood of winning. The commander who gets few scores during the calculations in the temple before the war will have less chance of success. With many scores, one can win; with few scores, one cannot. How much less chance of victory has one who gets no scores at all! By examining the situation through these aspects, I can foresee who is likely to win or lose.

北宋统一战争
The War of Unification in the Song Dynasty

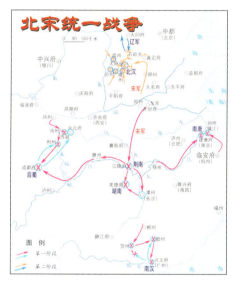

公元960年，刚建国的北宋皇帝赵匡胤和诸臣，针对南方的南唐、吴越、后蜀、南汉等割据势力较弱，又互不关联，而北方的北汉和辽国实力较强的形势，经过两年多反复酝酿，确定了先易后难、先南后北的战略方针。随后逐一攻灭、降服南方各割据势力，最后迫降北汉，统一天下。

《宋史·赵普传》记载赵匡胤雪夜访赵普，商讨统一战争的战略方针。

赵匡胤(公元927～976年)，即宋太祖，涿州(今属河北)人，政治家、军事家。善用人才，注重谋略，瓦解敌人，以智取胜。

赵匡胤雪夜访赵普　作者　苗再新

辽上京临潢府故城残垣，位于内蒙古赤峰市巴林左旗东北。

宋代武士俑

宋代箭镞

宋代衔枚

辽代铁刀

辽代车辖

金代武士石刻

桂陵之战
The Battle of Guiling

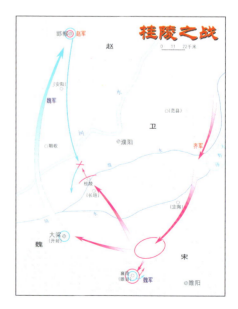

公元前353年，魏军攻赵，赵国向齐国求救。齐国经过庙算分析，决定待两国实力削弱后，再出兵攻魏救赵。不久，齐将田忌、军师孙膑率军8万乘魏都大梁空虚"围魏救赵"、"批亢捣虚"，迫使魏军回救，并于桂陵（今河南长垣西北）进行截击，一举将其歼灭。

孙膑，战国时期著名军事家。孙武后裔。创造"围魏救赵"战法，著有兵法。

《孙膑兵法》竹简（复制品）（银雀山汉墓竹简博物馆提供）

统兵用将的治军思想
The Thinking of Commanding the Army: leading the army and deploying the commanders

"卒未亲附而罚之，则不服，不服则难用也。卒已亲附而罚不行，则不可用也。故令之以文，齐之以武，是谓必取。"（行军篇）

If troops are punished before they have grown attached to you, they will be disobedient. If not obedient, it is difficult to employ them. If troops have become attached to you, but discipline is not enforced, you cannot employ them either. Thus, soldiers must be treated in the first instance with humanity, but kept under control by iron discipline. In this way, the allegiance of soldiers is assured.

"将者，智、信、仁、勇、严者也。"（计篇）

The commander stands for the general's qualities of wisdom, sincerity, benevolence, courage, and strictness.

令文齐武的统兵之法
Combination of Hardness and Tenderness in Commanding

成吉思汗(1162～1227年)，名铁木真，蒙古族，杰出的军事家，政治家。蒙古汉国的创始人，元太祖。他善于治军，创建和统帅的蒙古军，把一支由各部落组成的松散武装，建设成一支训练有素，纪律严明，既善野战，又能攻坚的强大军队。

《元史·兵志》关于成吉思汗编组各级宿卫军及蒙古军、探马赤军的记载

蒙古骑兵画像

成吉思汗统一漠北图

元代菱形铁刀(内蒙古博物馆提供)

元代武士俑

元代铁蒺藜(内蒙古博物馆提供)

元代菱形铁镞(内蒙古博物馆提供)
元代桦皮弓囊(内蒙古博物馆提供)

元代至正十一年铜火铳

铜鎏金龙纹马鞍(内蒙古博物馆提供)

元代窄沿式铁盔(内蒙古博物馆提供)

必备五德的用将之道
Five Virtues Required in Deploying Commanders

戚继光(1528~1588年)，字元敬，明朝名将，民族英雄，军事家。屡摧大敌，抗倭战功卓著。注重练兵，尤擅练将，把《孙子兵法》为将"五德"具体化为26条标准，培养出一批优秀将领。著有《纪效新书》、《练兵实纪》。

戚继光发明的虎蹲炮

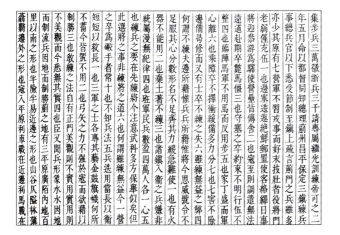

戚继光重视练将，提出"练兵之要在先练将"。图为《明史·戚继光传》有关戚继光论练兵、练将的记载。

明代北方水师基地蓬莱水城

明军抗倭图

明代金山岭长城障墙遗址

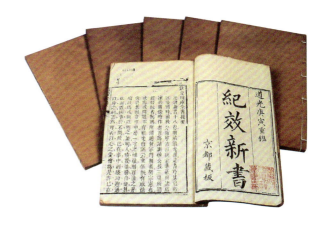

明代戚继光著《纪效新书·练将》

明代洪武十一年铜火铳

明代嘉靖二十四年子母铜火铳

明代武士俑

明代崇祯六年铁火炮

明代持长盾武士俑　　明代持圆盾武士俑

明弘治十八年碗口铳

明代冷兵器

"善用兵者，役不再籍，粮不三载；取用于国，因粮于敌，故军食可足也。"（作战篇）

Those adept in employing troops do not require a second levy of conscripts or more than two provisioning. They carry military supplies from the homeland and make up for their provisions relying on the enemy. Thus the army will be always plentifully provided.

"故智将务食于敌，食敌一钟，当吾二十钟；萁秆一石，当吾二十石。"（作战篇）

Hence a wise general is sure of getting provisions from the enemy countries. One zhong of grains obtained from local area is equal to twenty zhong shipped from the home country; one dan of fodder in the conquered area is equal to twenty dan from the domestic store.

清军收复新疆的战争
The War of recapturing Xin Jiang by the Qing Militay

1876年，左宗棠奉命指挥清军驱逐侵占新疆的阿古柏侵略军。由于路途遥远，除从内地运送粮草外，尤其注重从敌方夺取粮食。1877年，清军前方将领刘锦棠率部进入库尔勒，从敌军粮窖夺取粮食10余万斤，保障军队继续作战。清军逐步收复新疆，维护了祖国的领土完整。

因粮于敌　作者　苗再新

左宗棠（1812~1885年），字季高，湖南湘阴人。晚清军事家，湘军统帅，洋务派重要代表人物。

清代左宗棠印

清代鸟枪

清代黑皮鞘铜饰件腰刀

清代漆鞘铁宝剑

清代雕花玉柄钢刀

清代七星琴鹤剑

清代宝刀

清代威远将军炮

战国两色剑 长80厘米 宽4.2厘米
Double-colored Sword
Length, 80 cm; width, 4.2 cm

战国郾王喜矛　长 17.6 厘米　宽 3.5 厘米　河北省博物馆提供
Spear of Xi, King of the State of Yan, of the Period of Warring States
Length, 17.6 cm; width, 3.5 cm
Provided by Hebei Provincial Museum

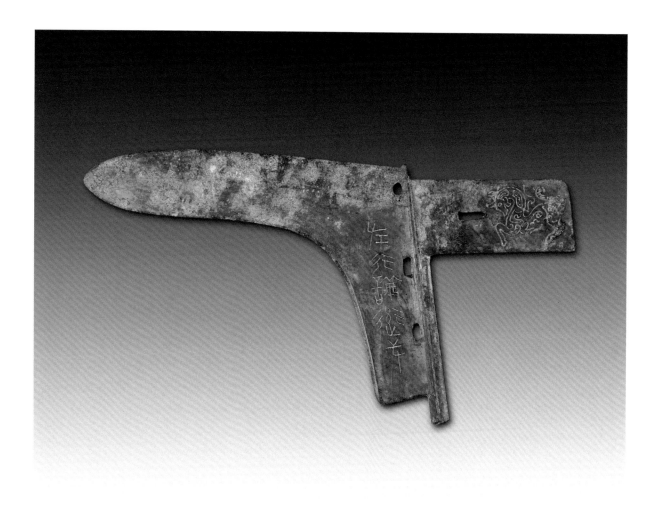

战国"左行议率"戈　通长21.6厘米　内长6.4厘米　河北省文物研究所提供
A dagger with the inscription of the words "zuo hang" of the Period of Warring states
Length, 21.6 cm
Provided by Hebei Research Institute for Cultural Heritage

秦弩机 长 8 厘米 高 16 厘米 宽 3.6 厘米 陕西临潼秦兵马俑坑出土
Crossbow Mechanism of Qin Dynasty
Length, 8 cm; Height, 16 cm; width, 3.6 cm
Excavated from Terra-Cotta Warriors Pit of Qin Dynasty in Lintong, Shaanxi Province

战国三戈戟　湖北随州曾侯乙墓出土　湖北省博物馆提供
Ternary Halberd of the Period of Warring States
Excavated from Zenghouyi Tomb in Suizhou, Hubei Province
Provided by Hubei Provincial Museum

战国铜戈 长 13.3 厘米 援长 8.9 厘米　内长 4.4 厘米　湖北随州曾侯乙墓出土　湖北省博物馆提供
Bronze Dagger of the Period of Warring States
Length, 13.3 cm
Excavated from Zenghouyi Tomb in Suizhou, Hubei Province
Provided by Hubei Provincial Museum

战国二戈戟 （上）长 27 厘米 援长 19 厘米 援宽 2.5 厘米（下）长 16.5 厘米 援长 15.4 厘米
援宽 2.1 厘米 湖北随州曾侯乙墓出土 湖北省博物馆提供

Dual Halber of the Period of Warring States

Length, 27 cm (top); length, 16.5 cm (bottom)

Excavated from Zenghouyi Tomb in Suizhou, Hubei Province

Provided by Hubei Provincial Museum

战国铜矛 长 12.55 厘米 筒径 1.7 厘米 湖北随州曾侯乙墓出土 湖北省博物馆提供
Bronze Spear of the Period of Warring States
Length, 12.55 cm; diameter (bottom), 1.7 cm
Excavated from Zenghouyi Tomb in Suizhou, Hubei Province
Provided by Hubei Provincial Museum

战国铜箭镞　湖北随州曾侯乙墓出土　湖北省博物馆提供
Bronze Arrowheads of the Period of Warring States
Excavated from Zenghouyi Tomb in Suizhou, Hubei Province
Provided by Hubei Provincial Museum

战国铜殳 长17.6厘米 銎径3厘米 湖北随州曾侯乙墓出土 湖北省博物馆提供
Bronze Pole Head of the Period of Warring States
Length, 17.6 cm; diameter (bottom), 3 cm
Excavated from Zenghouyi Tomb in Suizhou, Hubei Province
Provided by Hubei Provincial Museum

战国铜戈　河南省文物考古研究所提供
Bronze Pole Head of the Period of Warring States
Provided by Henan Research Institute for Cultural Heritage and Archaeology

战国三十三年郑令铍 长 31.8 厘米 宽 3.5 厘米 河南新郑县出土 河南博物院提供
Spear Head with the inscription of the words "thirty-third year, *Zheng Ling* and etc." of
the Period of Warring States
Length, 31.8 cm; width, 3.5 cm
Excavated from Xinzheng County, Henan Province
Provided by Henan Provincial Museum

战国素面薄格剑 长52厘米 宽4.7厘米 首径3.7厘米 河南博物院提供
Sword without inscription of the Period of Warring States
Length, 52 cm; width, 4.7 cm; bottom diameter, 3.7 cm
Provided by Henan Provincial Museum

战国兵避太岁戈　长21.9厘米　湖北荆门出土　荆州博物馆提供

Dagger with a pattern of a supermatual being

Length, 21.9 cm

Excavated from Jingmen, Hubei Province

Provided by Jingzhou Museum

战国铜矛　河南省文物考古研究所提供
Bronze Spear of the Period of Warring States
Provided by Henan Research Institute for Cultural Heritage and Archaeology

战国铜带钩　（上）长 11.6 厘米　　（下）长 11.7 厘米
Bronze Buckle of the Period of Warring States
Length, 11.6 cm (top); 11.7 cm (bottom)

相邦七年铜戟　矛　长15厘米　宽3.5厘米　戈　长26厘米　宽16.5厘米　秦兵马俑坑出土
Bronze Halberd, made in the 7th year of Xiangbang
Spear length, 15 cm; width 3.5 cm. Dagger length, 26 cm; width, 16.5 cm
Excavated from the Pit of Terra-Cotta Warriors of Qin Dynasty

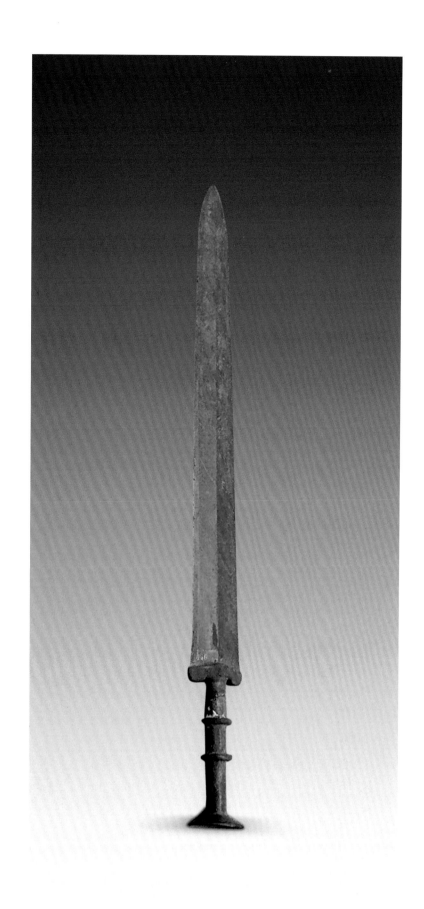

秦铜剑　长46厘米　宽4.2厘米　湖北云梦出土
Bronze Sword of Qin Dynasty
Length, 46 cm, width, 4.2 cm
Excavated from Yunmeng, Hubei Province

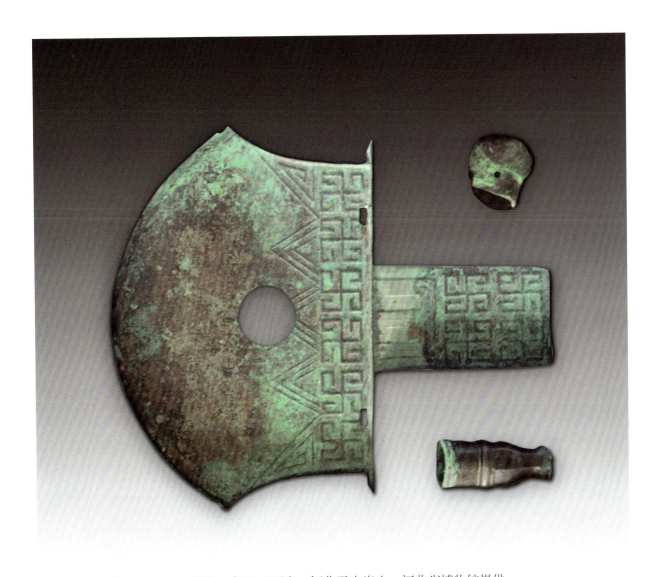

战国中山侯钺　长 29.6 厘米　宽 25.5 厘米　河北平山出土　河北省博物馆提供
Tomahawk of Marquis Zhongshan of the Period of Warring State
Length, 29.6 cm; width, 25.5 cm
Excavated in Ping Shan, Hebei Province
Provided by Hebei Provincial Museum

战国双钺形铜戈　长20.5厘米　宽18厘米　昆明市呈贡县出土　云南省博物馆提供
Double-Headed Axe of the Period of Warring States
Length, 20.5 cm; width, 18 cm
Excavated from Chenggong County, Kunming
Provided by Yunnan Provincial Museum

汉代陶带扣范　高 28 厘米　直径 13 厘米　河南省温县出土　河南博物院提供
Pottery Buckle Mold of Han Dynasty
Height, 28 cm; diameter, 13 cm
Excavated from Wen County, Henan Province
Provided by Henan Provincial Museum

汉代铜弩机 Bronze Crossbow Mechanism of Han Dynasty

建武三十二年铜弩机 河北省文物研究所提供
Bronze Crossbow Mechanism of Jianwu 32nd Year (56 AD)
Provided by Henan Research Institute for Cultural Heritage and Archaeology

东汉手搏画像砖　长 99 厘米　宽 41.5 厘米　高 13.5 厘米　南阳市文物考古研究所提供
Brick with Pictures of Hand-to-Hand Combat made in the Eastern Han Dynasty
Length, 99 cm; width, 41.5 cm; height, 13.5 cm
Provided by Nanyang Municipal Museum, Henan Province

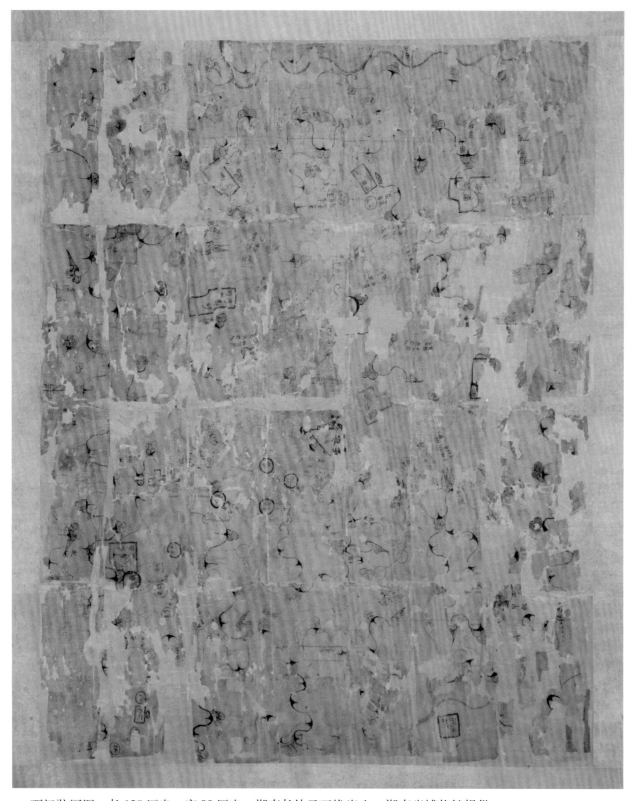

西汉驻军图　长 128 厘米　宽 99 厘米　湖南长沙马王堆出土　湖南省博物馆提供

Map of Garrison of Western Han Dynasty

Length, 128 cm; width, 99 cm

Excavated from Mawangdui Tomb in Changsha, Hunan Province

Provided by Hunan Provincial Museum

西汉驻军图局部
Part of Map of Garrison

西汉战争贮贝器　高 53.9 厘米　盖径 33 厘米　底径 37 厘米　云南晋宁出土　云南省博物馆提供
The War-Pictured Container for Storing Shell Money made in Western Han Dynasty
Height, 53.9 cm; top diameter, 33 cm; bottom diameter, 37 cm
Excavated in Jinning, Yunnan Province
Provided by Yunnan Provincial Museum

西汉战争贮贝器盖
Lid of the War-Pictured Container for Storing Shell Money

西汉彩绘骑马俑　高 68 厘米　长 63 厘米　咸阳杨家湾出土　咸阳博物馆提供
Cavalry Figurine with Colored Loricae, made in Western Han Dynasty
Height, 68 cm; Length, 63 cm
Excavated from Yangjiawan, Xianyang
Provided by Xianyang Municipal Museum

西汉彩绘带冠红衣长甲扛械俑　高 49 厘米
宽 14 厘米　咸阳杨家湾出土　咸阳博物馆提供
Infantry Figurine shouldering weapon with Colored
Loricae, made in Western Han Dynasty
Height, 49 cm; width, 14 cm
Excavated from Yangjiawan, Xianyang
Provided by Xianyang Municipal Museum

西汉步兵俑　高 50 厘米　宽 15 厘米
Infantry Figurine of Western Han Dynasty
Height, 50 cm; width, 15 cm

东汉胡汉战争画像砖　长122厘米　宽14厘米　高33厘米　河南新野出土　河南博物院提供

Brick with Picture of Battles between Hu Nationality and Han Nationality

Length, 122 cm; width, 14 cm; height, 33 cm

Excavated from Xinye, Henan Province

Provided by Nanyang Municipal Museum, Henan Province

三国撞车头　长17厘米　宽4厘米
Head of the Shoving Chariot made in the period of Three Kingdoms
Length, 17 cm; width, 4 cm

三国部曲将印　长2.4厘米　宽2.4厘米　高2.1厘米
Senior General's Signet made in the period of Three Kingdoms
Length, 2.4 cm; width, 2.4 cm; height, 2.1 cm

三国部曲将印　长2.4厘米　宽2.4厘米　高2.1厘米
Senior General's Signet made in the period of Three Kingdoms
Length, 2.4 cm; width, 2.4 cm; height, 2.1 cm

三国铁镞
Iron Arrowheads of the period of Three Kingdoms

三国铁镞范　长 22.5 厘米　宽 19.5 厘米　河南渑池出土　河南博物院提供
Iron Mold for Making Arrowhead of the period of Three Kingdoms
Length, 22.5 cm; width 19.5 cm
Excavated from Mianchi, Henan Province
Provided by Henan Provincial Museum

西晋骑俑　长16厘米　高24厘米　湖南长沙金盆岭出土
Cavalry Figurine of Western Jin Dynasty
Length, 16 cm; height, 24 cm
Excavated in Jinpen Ridge, Changsha, Hunan Province

魏晋南北朝负箭箙俑　高24.5厘米　宽7.5厘米
A Figurine of a soldier carrying a arrow bag, made
in Wei and Jin Dynasties and the Southern and
Northern Dynasties
Height, 24.5 cm; width, 7.5 cm

魏晋南北朝套衣风帽侍卫俑　高 24.8 厘米
宽 7.5 厘米
A bodyguard Figurine, made in Wei and Jin
Dynasties and the Southern and Northern Dynasties
Height, 24.8 cm; width, 7.5 cm

魏晋南北朝负箭箙小冠俑　高 24.5 厘米
宽 8.5 厘米
A Figurine of a soldier carrying a arrow bag, made
in Wei and Jin Dynasties and the Southern and
Northern Dynasties
Height, 24.5 cm; width, 8.5 cm

魏晋南北朝高领长甲侍卫俑　高 25.5 厘米
宽 7.5 厘米
A bodyguard Figurine, made in Wei and Jin
Dynasties and the Southern and Northern Dynasties
Height, 24.8 cm; width, 7.5 cm

北朝武士俑　高 25.5 厘米　宽 7.5 厘米　河南安阳张庄出土
Warrior Figurine of Northern Dynasties
Height, 25.5 cm; width, 7.5 cm
Excavated in Zhang County, Anyang, Henan Province

西晋持盾武士俑　高 19 厘米　宽 11 厘米　湖南长沙金盆岭出土
Warrior Figurine Holding Shied of Western Jin Dynasty
Height, 19 cm; width,11cm
Excavated in Jinpen Ridge, Changsha, Hunan Province

隋代虎符　高 4.5 厘米　长 7.5 厘米　甘肃庄浪出土
Tiger-shaped Tally of Sui Dynasty
Height, 4.5 cm; length, 7.5 cm
Excavated in Zhuanglang, Gansu Province

唐代彩绘贴金甲马骑兵俑　高36厘米　陕西乾县懿德太子墓出土　陕西历史博物馆提供
Cavalry Figurine with Colored and Gilded Loricae, made in Tang Dynasty
Height, 36 cm
Excavated in Qian County, Shaanxi Province
Provided by Shaanxi History Museum

唐代三彩骑射俑　高 38 厘米　宽 32 厘米
Tricolor Shooting Cavalry Figurine of Tang Dynasty
Height, 38 cm; width, 32 cm

唐代彩绘红陶虎头帽武士俑　高 32 厘米　宽 11 厘米　昭陵陪葬墓尉迟敬德墓出土
昭陵博物馆提供
Warrior Figurine with Colored Loricae of Tang Dynasty　Height, 32 cm; width, 11 cm
Excavated from the Tomb of Yuchi Jingde, burried beside the Zhao Mausoleum
Provided by the Museum of Zhao Mausoleum

唐代粉彩金甲武士俑　高 30 厘米　宽 10 厘米　陕西段氏墓出土
Warrior Figurine with Colored and Gilded Armor, made in Tang Dynasty
Height, 30 cm; width, 10 cm
Excavated from Duan's Tomb, Shaanxi Province

宋代武士俑　高 33 厘米　宽 11.5 厘米
Warrior Figurine of Song Dynasty
Height, 33 cm; width, 11.5 cm

元代武士俑　高30厘米　宽14厘米
Warrior Figurine of Yuan Dynasty
Height, 30 cm; width, 14 cm

明代武士俑　高55.5厘米　宽20厘米
Warrior Figurine of Ming Dynasty
Height, 55.5 cm; width, 20 cm

铜鎏金龙纹马鞍 内蒙古博物馆提供
Gold-plating Copper Saddle with the Dragon Pattern
Provided by the Inner Mongolia Museum

元代窄沿式铁盔　　高45厘米　　底径26.5厘米　　内蒙古锡林郭勒盟正蓝旗出土　　内蒙古博物馆提供
Iron Helmet of Yuan Dynasty
Height, 45 cm; bottom diameter, 26.5 cm
Exccavated from Xilinguole, Inner Mongolia
Provided by Inner Mongolia Museum

明代持长盾武士俑　高21厘米　宽9.5厘米
Warrior Figurine Holding Long Shield of Ming
Dynasty
Height, 21 cm; width, 9.5 cm

明代持圆盾武士俑　高21厘米　宽7.5厘米
Warrior Figurine Holding Round Shield of Ming
Dynasty
Height, 21 cm; width, 7.5 cm

明弘治十八年碗口铳　长24厘米　口径6厘米
Small Artillery, Made in the 18th Year of Hongzhi, Ming Dynasty
Length, 24 cm; caliber, 6cm

元代至正十一年铜火铳　长43厘米　口径3厘米
Copper Tubiform Gun, Made in the 11th Year of Zhizheng, Yuan Dynasty
Length, 43cm; caliber, 3cm

明代洪武十一年铜火铳　长44厘米　口径2厘米
Copper Tubiform Gun, made in the 11th year of Hongwu, Ming Dynasty
Length, 44 cm; caliber, 2 cm

明代嘉靖二十四年子·母铜火铳　母铳　长63厘米　口径2.2厘米
　　　　　　　　　　　　　　　　子铳　长15.5厘米　口径1.6厘米
Composite Tubiform Gun, made in the 24th year of Jiajing, Ming Dynasty
Length, 63 cm; caliber, 2.2 cm (outer)
Length, 15.5 cm; caliber, 1.6 cm (inner)

明代崇祯六年铁火炮　长150厘米　口径6.5厘米
Iron cannon, made in the 6th year of Chongzhen, Ming Dynasty
Length, 150 cm; caliber, 6.5 cm

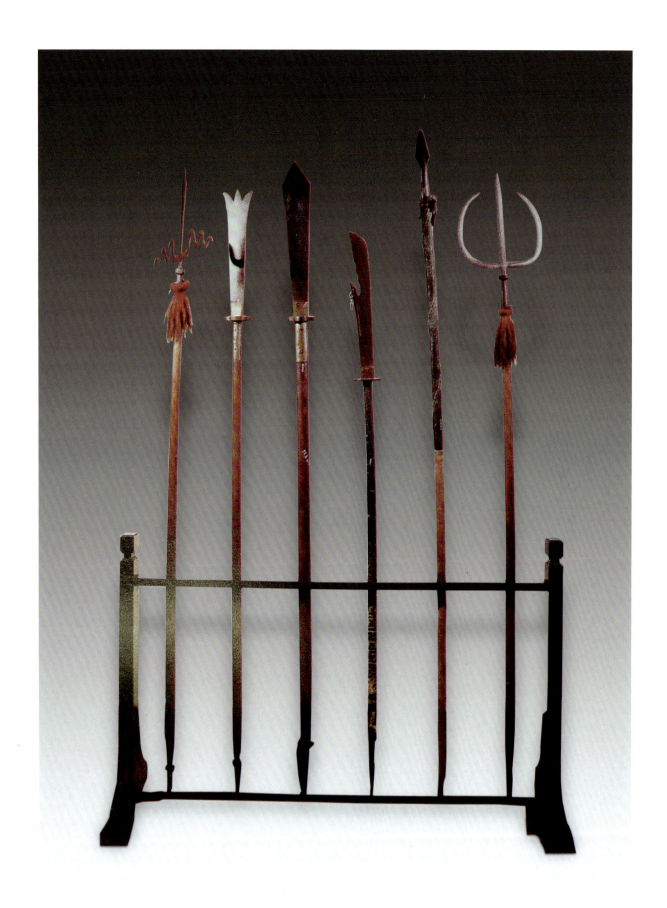

明代冷兵器
Cold Weapon of Ming Dynasty

清代左宗棠印
General Zuo Zongtang's signet of Qing Dynasty

清代鸟枪　长 153 厘米　口径 1.2 厘米
Fowling Piece of Qing Dynasty
Length, 153 cm; caliber, 1.2 cm

清代黑皮鞘铜饰件腰刀　长 86.5 厘米　宽 8.5 厘米
Broadsword with Black Leather Scabbard and Copper Decorations, made in Qing Dynasty
Length, 86.5 cm; width, 8.5 cm

清代雕花玉柄钢刀　长 49.5 厘米　宽 5.5 厘米
Steel Knife with a Jade Handle Carved with Flowers, made in Qing Dynasty
Length, 49.5 cm; width, 5.5 cm

清代漆鞘铁宝剑　长91厘米　宽8.6厘米
Iron Sword with Lacquered Scabbard, made in Qing Dynasty
Length, 91 cm; width, 8.6 cm

清代宝刀　长 90.5 厘米　宽 7.5 厘米
Treasured Sword of Qing Dynasty
Length, 90.5 cm; width, 7.5 cm

清代七星琴鹤剑　长 91.5 厘米　宽 8.5 厘米
Sword Decorated with the Big Dipper, Zither and Crane Patterns,
made in Qing Dynasty
Length, 91.5 cm; width, 8.5 cm

清代威远将军炮　长 104 厘米　口径 21 厘米
General Weiyuan Cannon of Qing Dynasty
Length, 104 cm; caliber0, 21 cm

第三部分 兵学哲理 魅力永存
Part Three Ever-lasting Glamour of the Military Philosophies

《孙子兵法》历数千年而不衰，具有超越时空的生命力，根本原因是它体现了朴素的唯物论和辩证法，立足于军事实践，揭示了战争的一般规律。它不仅被中国历代兵家奉为至上经典，其思想价值在当代也得到东西方的普遍认同，正可谓"后孙子者，不能遗孙子"。

The fundamental reason why The Art of War could transcend thousands of years and maintain its everlasting vigor is that it embodies the basic principles of dialectical materialism and reveals the typical rules of war on the basis of military activities. It is held as the supreme masterpiece by the military through out ancient Chinese history. In addition, the value of its thoughts is well recognized by both the East and West in modern times. As the comment goes, the military strategies before Sun Tzu were all summarized in this book and all the military strategies devised after Sun Tzu are all inseparable from this book.

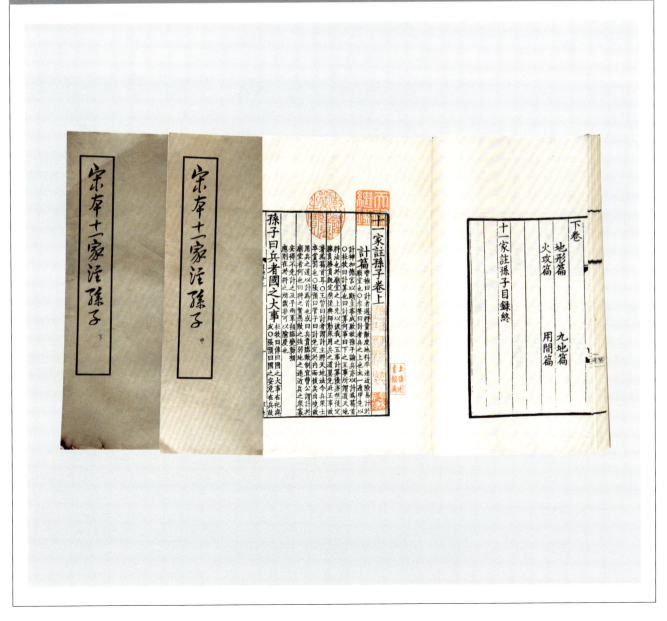

《孙子兵法》的传播和影响
Spreading and Impact of The Art of War

《孙子兵法》的传播
The Spreading of The Art of War

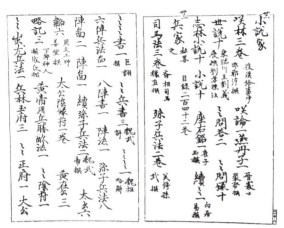

在中国唐朝时期，日本遣唐学生吉备真备（公元693～775）将《孙子兵法》带回日本（有日本学者认为，早在中国魏晋时期已传到日本），受到日本兵学界的重视。图为公元9世纪藤原佐世著录了6种《孙子兵法》的《日本国见在书目》。

钱德明（Joseph Marie Amiot, 1718～1793年），法国来华传教士。

武田信玄（1521～1573年），日本战国时代的名将。

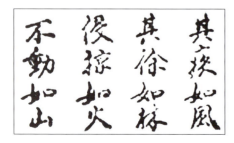

武田信玄十分推崇《孙子兵法》，将书中"其疾如风，其徐如林，侵掠如火，不动如山"16个字绣在军旗上。这些军旗被日本人称为"孙子之旗"，现保存在日本盐山市云峰寺。

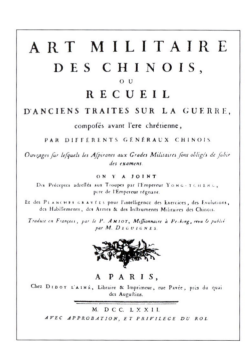

1772年，钱德明把《孙子兵法》等4部中国古代军事著作译成法文，以《中国军事艺术》之名在巴黎出版。此后俄、英、德、意大利、西班牙、葡萄牙文等《孙子兵法》译本纷纷问世。图为该书书影。

钱德明1793年在北京去世。图为其墓碑拓片。

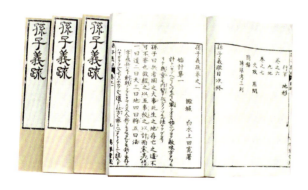

1771年日文版《孙子义疏》

《孙子兵法》的当代影响
The Influence of The Art of War in Modern Times

《孙子兵法》在当代产生了世界范围的广泛影响。1989年中国孙子兵法研究会成立,定期召开国际学术讨论会,至今已举办7届。图为第七届孙子兵法国际研讨会会场。

1960年英国蒙哥马利元帅访华,向毛泽东主席建议世界各国军事院校都应该开设《孙子兵法》课。图为毛泽东主席会见蒙哥马利的照片。

中国邀请国外学者研讨《孙子兵法》

国防大学研究生孙子兵法教学基地

江苏苏州吴中孙武书院

中国孙子兵法学者赴国外进行学术交流，在外国军事院校讲授《孙子兵法》。

广东深圳孙子研究会成立大会

中国孙子兵法研究会

山东临沂银雀山汉墓竹简博物馆

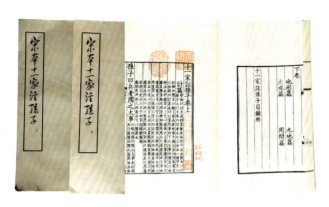

《宋本十一家注孙子》（影印本）

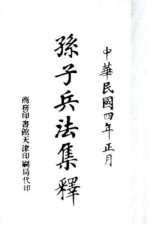

民国本《孙子兵法集释》

《孙子十家注》

孙子兵法传世典藏本

《孙子释证》

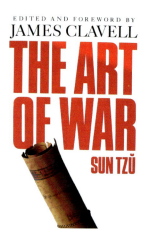

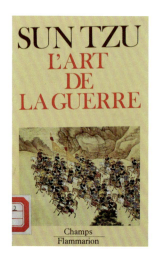

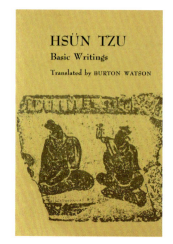

各种外文版本《孙子兵法》

竹简《孙子兵法》（复制品）

微雕《孙子兵法》

丝绸版《孙子兵法》

黄金版《孙子兵法》

历届孙子兵法国际研讨会论文集

《孙子兵法》的现代评价
Evaluation of The Art of War at Modern Times

毛泽东（1893~1976年），社会主义新中国和中国人民解放军主要创建人和领导人，杰出的军事理论家和军事指挥家。

中国古代大军事学家孙武子书上"知彼知己，百战不殆"这句话，是包括学习和使用两个阶段而说的，包括从认识客观实际中的发展规律，并按照这些规律去决定自己行动克服当前敌人而说的；我们不要看轻这句话。

孙子的规律，"知彼知己，百战不殆"，仍是科学的真理。

孙中山（1866~1925年），中国资产阶级民主革命先行者，推翻清朝统治武昌起义的决策者，中华民国的创始人。

就中国历史来考究，二千多年前的兵书有十三篇，那十三篇兵书便是解释当时的战理。由于那十三篇兵书，便成立中国的军事哲学。

B.H.利德尔·哈特（Liddellhart1895~1970年），英国军事理论家。

刘伯承（1892~1986年），中国人民解放军创建人和领导人，军事家。

《孙子兵法》这部兵法，是研究指导战争最普遍规律的著作。

正兵和奇兵，是辩证的统一，是为将者必须掌握的重要法则。奇中有正，正中有奇，奇正相生，变化无穷。

孙子兵法是世界上最早的军事名作。其内容之博大，论述之精深，后世无出其右者。可以说，《孙子兵法》是有关战争指导的智慧之结晶。历数古往今来的军事思想家，只有克劳塞维茨堪与孙子伦比；然而他的著作时代局限性大，而且有一部分已经过时，尽管他是在孙子之后两千多年写的。相比之下，孙子的文章讲得更透彻、更深刻，永远给人以新鲜感。

第四部分 古代军事专题
Part Four Special Subjects of Ancient Military Affairs

弓弩是人类战争史上最早出现的远射武器。铠甲是冷兵器战争时代将士披挂在身上的防护装具。相传黄帝发明指南车，并用于对蚩尤的作战。战国时期发明了以天然磁石制作的指南仪器"司南"。公元10世纪开始，中国军事家根据炼丹家发明的火药配方，创制了燃烧性火器、爆炸性火器、管形射击火器、反推作用火箭等。中国古代军事指挥最初由指挥员用语言和动作直接下命令，后来出现了旌旗鼓角等通信指挥工具⋯⋯

Bow/Crossbow is the earliest weapon used for long distance shooting in the history of war. Armor was used by the soldiers to protect themselves in the cold weapon era. According to the legend, it was Emperor Huang who invented the compass cart, which was used in the battles with Chiyou. During the Warring States period, there appeared another direction indicating device called "Sinan" (south-pointing ladle), made of magnet. In the 10th century, Chinese military strategists, on the basis of the gunpowder formula contrived by alchemists, had developed flammable devices, explosive devices, tube firing devices, and retro-rocket etc. In ancient China, the commanders at first issued their orders directly in words and body language. Later, there appeared communicating and commanding tools such as banners, drums and horns.

弓弩与远射
Bow/Crossbow and Long Distance Shooting

弓弩是人类战争史上最早出现的远射武器。弓由带有弹性的弓臂和弓弦构成，开弓时所产生的张力可将扣在弦上的箭或弹丸射向目标。弩将弓装在弩臂上，并增加了可供瞄准和控弦的弩机，因而可延时发射。战国时期出现的带廓青铜弩机，使弩成为一种更强有力的杀伤武器。中国古代发明的弩曾先后两次传入欧洲，对西方战争史上十字军东征等战争产生了深远的影响。

Bow/Crossbow is the earliest weapon used for long distance shooting in the history of war. A bow consists of a flexible arch and a string. With the tension generated by pulling, it can launch the arrow or the projectile clung to the string toward the target. The crossbow includes an arch fixed to the center spine, and a trigger mechanism was added to it, which can facilitate targeting and retaining the string, so as to make delay firing. A kind of bronze crossbow with casing was invented during the Warring States period, thus adding greater power to this weapon for killing. The crossbow invented by ancient China had been introduced to Europe twice and exerted profound influence on the Crusade in the western history of war.

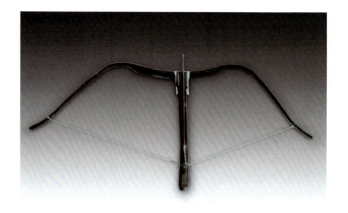

战国弩臂为木制，弩机为青铜所制，弩弓用竹制。

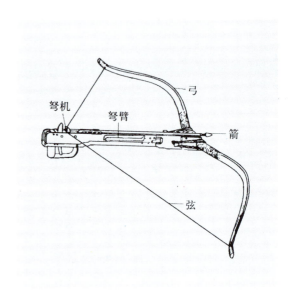

战国弩结构示意图

春秋竹弓　弓臂用单根竹材弯曲而成，称为单体弓。春秋时期出现了用多种材料制成的复合弓。

唐代高昌弓箭

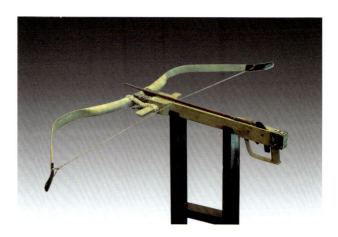

汉代弩是抗击匈奴的重要武器，广泛使用"擘张弩"、"蹶张弩"，还发明了"腰引弩"，其弓力更强，更具杀伤力。

战国时代发明了可以双箭齐射的连弩，提高了发射速度。此为湖北江陵战国楚墓出土的连弩。（荆州博物馆提供）

汉代刻度铜弩机　有廓，在望山上增加了刻度，弓力更强，瞄准更加精确，命中率更高。

三国时诸葛亮改进连弩，创制了元戎连弩，其箭匣装置，减少了装箭的时间，提高了射击速度。

汉代鎏金铜弩机

床弩是一种将一张弓或几张弓安于床架上、利用绞动轮轴射箭的大型弩，其威力更强，为攻守城重器。图为复原的宋代三弓床弩。

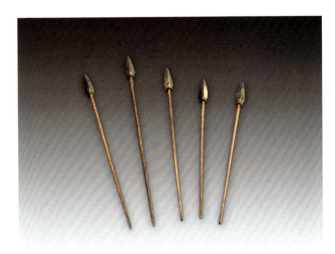

秦青铜三棱箭镞，表面经过特殊防锈处理，形制十分规整划一。

铠甲与防护
Armor and Physical Protection

铠甲是冷兵器战争时代将士披挂在身上的防护装具。早期主要以皮革制造，称之为"甲"；后来用青铜和铁制造，称之为"铠"。魏晋南北朝时期，骑兵作战十分频繁，出现了人和马都披铠甲的重装甲骑兵——"甲骑具装"。火药武器用于战争后，铠甲逐步走向衰落。

Armor was used by the soldiers to protect themselves in the cold weapon era. It was first mainly made of leather, so it was called armor. Later on, bronze and iron was used, and then it was called loricae. During the Wei-Jin period and the Southern and Northern Dynasties, the cavalry were frequently deployed in the war, which result in the armored cavalry—"both the soldiers and horses were heavily armored". Ever since gunpowder weapons were used in the war, the armor gradually became out of use.

各异的甲片，表面涂漆，然后利用甲片上的穿孔，用绳编联成可以部分活动的皮甲。图为复原的战国皮甲，在车战中与盾相配合，能有效地防御青铜兵器的攻击。

布依族藤甲胄，保存了较为原始的甲胄形态，用藤条编织而成，并浸渍桐油，以增强防护能力。我国台湾兰屿耶美人亦用藤甲。

商周时期开始出现的皮甲，将皮革裁成大小不同、形状

战国晚期出现了铁制铠甲，至汉代铁铠成为军队的主要防护装具。西汉时期的铁铠，从较大长条形甲片编联的"札甲"逐渐发展到用较小甲片制成的"鱼鳞甲"；由仅有保护胸、背的形式，发展到有保护肩臂、腰胯的部分，甚至出现了能保护面部的"面衣"和保护腿部的"裙甲"。

河北满城西汉中山靖王刘胜墓铁甲，有保护肩臂的"披膊"和保护腰胯的"垂缘"的鱼鳞甲，由2859片甲片编成，重16.85千克。

清代绵甲胄　用棉布和棉花制成，并饰有排列整齐的金属泡钉，以增强防护效能。绵甲轻便，并能防御早期火器所发射弹丸的伤害，故在明清时期较为流行。

清代铁盔锁子甲

锁子甲是一种有许多金属环套扣而成的铠甲，东晋时传自西域，至唐代成为军队制式装备。用精铁打制的锁子甲，轻软坚密，具有较强的防护能力。

指南针的发明和使用
Invention and Use of Compass

相传黄帝发明指南车，并用于对蚩尤的作战。战国时期发明了以天然磁石制作的指南仪器"司南"。宋代水法罗盘和旱罗盘技术发展成熟，12世纪经阿拉伯传播到欧洲。指南针是中国古代四大发明之一，对世界军事和航海技术的发展产生了相当深远的影响。

According to the legend, it was Emperor Huang who invented the compass cart, which was used in the battles with Chiyou. During the Warring States period, there appeared another direction indicating device called "Sinan" (south-pointing ladle), made of magnet. In the Song Dynasty, the technology of floating compass and land compass became mature and was introduced to Europe in the 12th century through Arabic countries. Compass is one of the Four Great Inventions of Ancient China and has far reaching impact on the development of world military activities and navigating technology.

悬挂式指南针

司南是指南针的始祖，它由天然磁石琢成勺形放在青铜铸成的"地盘"之上，磁勺能顺应地球磁场指向南北。

北宋沈括《梦溪笔谈》记载的磁性指向仪器之一。以天然磁石摩擦钢针使之磁化，并横贯灯芯浮于水面。是一种简单实用的指南针。

北宋《武经总要》记载的天阴下雨部队行军所用指南鱼，用薄铁片裁成鱼形，利用地磁和热剩磁效应使之磁化，浮在水面即能指南。

《韩非子》关于司南的记载

中国古代的一种机械定向装置。传说最早由黄帝发明，即应用于战争。三国魏机械专家马钧、南北朝科学家祖冲之曾重复发明制造。此为据《宋史》记载复原制作的北宋燕肃指南车。

南宋时发明了将磁针装在方位盘上的旱罗盘。此为江西临川南宋墓出土的持罗盘仙人俑。

罗盘

郑和下西洋船队使用有24方位的水浮式航海罗盘。图为《武备志》（1621年）所载郑和下西洋针路图。

《中山传信录》（1720年）载清远洋航船"封舟"，船尾专门设有以指南针导航的"针房"。

公元10世纪开始，中国军事家根据炼丹家发明的火药配方，创制了燃烧性火器、爆炸性火器、管形射击火器、反推作用火箭等，用于作战，从而开始了人类战争史上火器与冷兵器并用的时代。

In the 10th century, Chinese military strategists, on the basis of the gunpowder formula contrived by alchemists, had developed flammable devices, explosive devices, tube firing devices, and retro-rocket etc. for military operations. This ushered in the era of employing both hot weapons and cold weapons in the history of war.

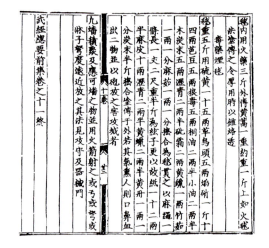

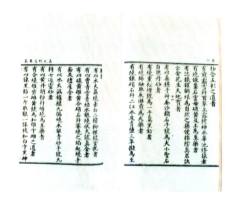

唐代中期以后成书的炼丹著作《真元妙道要略》记载了火药燃烧现象。

中国古代发明的黑火药由硫磺、硝石、木炭等组成的混合物，是人类最早发明的一种自供氧燃烧体系。

北宋《武经总要》记载了世界上最早的火药配方以及爆炸性火器的制造方法。

敦煌莫高窟五代绢画《降魔变》中的喷火兵器

《宋史》等文献中关于使用火枪的记载

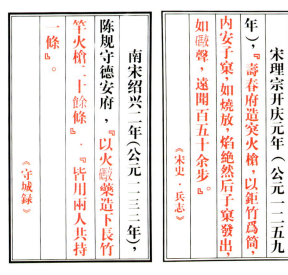

引火球，燃烧性火器，点燃后投至敌军。

竹火鷂，燃烧性火器。用竹编成篓状，外糊纸数层，内填火药及小卵石，一端装有干草，点燃后用抛石机投向敌军。

蒺藜火球，爆炸性火器。以铁蒺藜为核心，外敷火药，周身安插倒须钉，抛至目标，烧杀敌人。

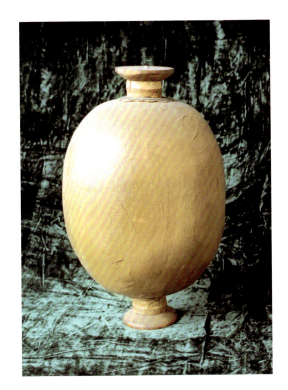

霹雳火球，爆炸性火器。竹节中装薄瓷片和火药，外糊纸壳成"亞"形，引燃后投至敌军，声如霹雳。

火箭，中国古代发明的依靠火药燃气反推作用飞行的武器。

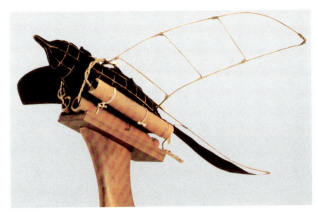

神火飞鸦，是一种多火药筒并联火箭。

147

一窝蜂，是一种多发齐射火箭武器。

火龙出水，是一种二级火箭，增加了武器的飞行距离。

军事通信
Military Communication

中国古代军事指挥最初由指挥员用语言和动作直接下命令，后来出现了旌旗鼓角等通信指挥工具。西周时期出现了传递军情和边塞警报的烽燧和邮驿。中国古代也最早应用了信鸽、火药爆炸等军事通信工具。

In ancient China, the commanders at first issued their orders directly in words and body language. Over time, the communication commanding devices came into being, such as banners, drums and horns. The Western Zhou Dynasty (11th century BC to 711 BC) witnessed the signal fire and post-horse used for transmitting military intelligence and alarms at the frontier. Other devices such as homing pigeon and explosive powder were also used in ancient China for military communication.

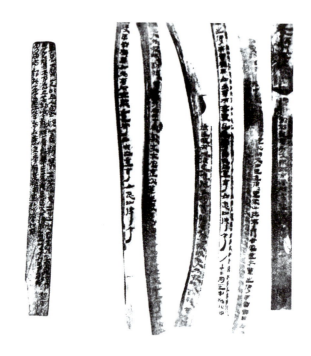

竹简汉代烽火品约，记载了汉代烽燧传递军情警报的原则和规定，标志着汉代已形成严密的烽燧通信制度。

烽燧，又称烽火台，是通过烟火信号传递军情警报的设施。

积薪和苇苣均是烽燧所用燃料，用以点火或举烟传递报警信号。

好水川之战中，西夏军设伏诱宋军入围，百余只带鸽哨的家鸽自盒中飞起，为夏军发出合击信号，大败宋军。这是中国历史上信鸽用于军事通信的较早记录。

商代大铜铙　军乐器，槌击而鸣，以鼓舞士气。

驿站是古代专门传递军事情报的机构，通过人或马匹接力送递军事文书。图为鸡鸣驿城址。

战国铜钲　古代军事指挥中的"鸣金"即为敲击钲所发出的信号。

潼关以备衝突秋夏人轉攻河東及麟府不能下乃引
震動都監李禹亨劉均皆死於陣觀以千餘人保民傳陳將李
簡與監軍步兵大潰泉遂奔珪英津及羕軍耿傅陳將盜
矢四射會暮夏軍引去將校士卒死者萬三百人關右
至東陣歩兵不可動英重傷不能出軍戰自午至申夏軍盜
陣陣堅不可動英重傷不能出軍戰自午至申夏軍三
遇陳合王珪自羊牧隆城以屯兵四千五百人助觀畧
千餘為諸將後繼是日朱觀武英東會能家川與夏人
密中有動躍飛軍上於是夏兵四合懌先犯中軍繼自
既而鮑老揮左則右伏出揮左則左懌没小校劉進勘福自
師大敗懌蕭及福子懷亮皆戰夏亭塞騎兵三
自辰至午酣戰陣中忽樹鮑老旗長二丈餘懌而襲
五里與夏軍遇懌為先鋒見道傍置數銀泥合封籠謹
多兵葢進詰旦福與懌循好水川西去未至羊牧隆城
欽定四庫全書　宋史卷四百八十五

《宋史・夏国传》记载了北宋庆历元年（1041 年）宋夏

铜鼓　西南少数民族特有的乐器，鼓声宏大辽远，战时也用来传播指挥信号。

汉代虎钮錞钎　用绳系钮悬于架上，响声如雷，战场上用于号令军士进退。

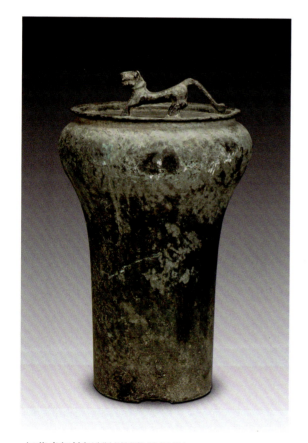

鸣镝　北方契丹民族使用的能发出声音的响箭，战时可传递军事信息。

汉代虎钮錞钎（荆州博物馆提供）

清代四眼铳　常用于作战，并用作信号枪。

战国双箭齐射连弩　长 27.8 厘米　高 17.2 厘米　宽 5 .4 厘米　湖北江陵秦家嘴楚墓出土
Repeating crossbow, which could launch two arrows at a time, of the Period of Warring State
Length, 27.8 cm; height, 17.2 cm; width, 5.4 cm
Excavated from a tomb of the State of Chu, Qinjiazui, Jiangling, Hubei province

战国连弩残件
Relics of the Repeating Crossbow of the Period of Warring State

弩箭（复制品）
Bolts (replicates)

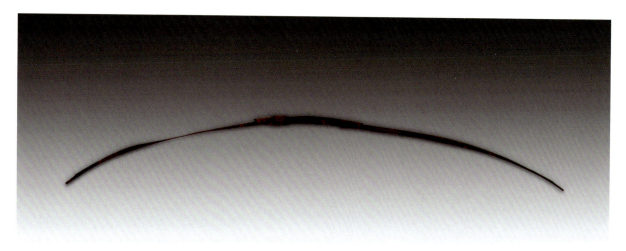

春秋竹弓　长 112 厘米
Bamboo Bow of the Spring and Autumn Period
Length, 112 cm

唐代高昌弓箭　弓长 80.5 厘米　箭长 93.5 厘米
Gaochang Bow of Tang Dynasty
Length of Bow, 80.5 cm; Length of Arrow, 93.5 cm

汉代鎏金铜弩机　长 15.4 厘米　高 16.5 厘米
Gold-plating Bronze Crossbow Mechanism of Han Dynasty
Length, 15.4 cm; width, 16.5 cm

汉代刻度铜弩机　长 18 厘米　高 21 厘米
Bronze Crossbow Mechanism with Scales of Han Dynasty
Length, 18 cm; width 21 cm

清代铁盔锁子甲　铁盔　高28厘米　通径27厘米　　锁子甲　高 84厘米　宽65厘米
Iron Helmet and Chain Armor of Qing Dynasty
Iron Helmet: height, 28 cm; diameter, 27 cm
Chain Armor: height, 84 cm; width, 65 cm

清代绵甲　高 198 厘米　宽 179.5 厘米
Padded Armor of Qing Dynasty
Height, 198 cm; width, 179.5 cm

战国皮甲胄（复原）

Leather Armor and Helmet of the Period of Warring State (restored)

汉代铁甲胄（复原）
Iron Armor and Helmet of Han Dynasty (restored)

汉代铁甲胄（复原）
Iron Armor and Helmet of Han Dynasty (restored)

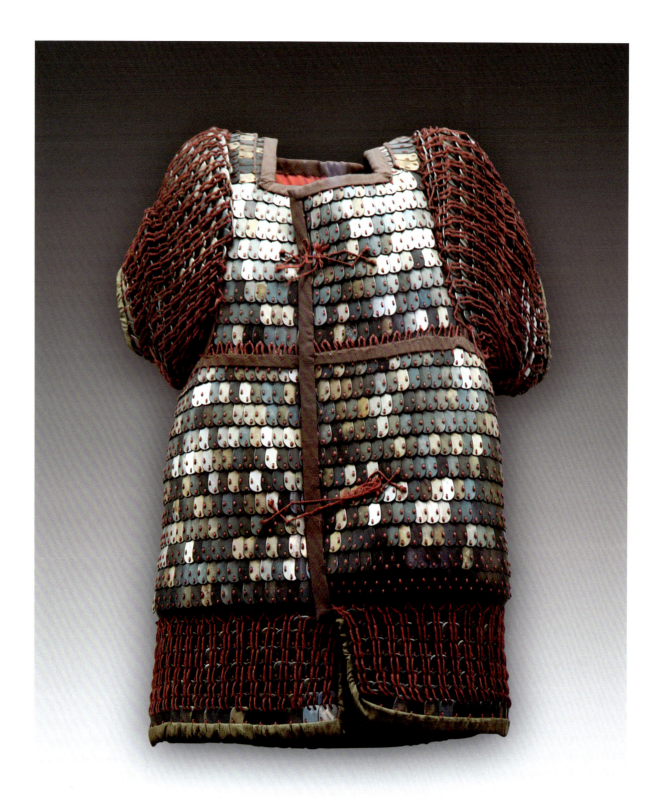

汉代铁甲胄（复原）
Iron Armor and Helmet of Han Dynasty (restored)

南宋持罗盘俑　高 23.5 厘米

A Figurine holding a compass of Southern Song Dynasty

Height, 23.5 cm

商代大铜铙　高 69 厘米　直径 50 厘米
Bronze Cymbal of Shang Dynasty
Height, 69 cm; diameter, 50 cm

战国铜钲　高 41.5 厘米　口径 12.5 厘米
Bronze *Zheng* (bell-shaped drum) of the Period of Warring State
Height, 41.5 cm; diameter, 12.5 cm

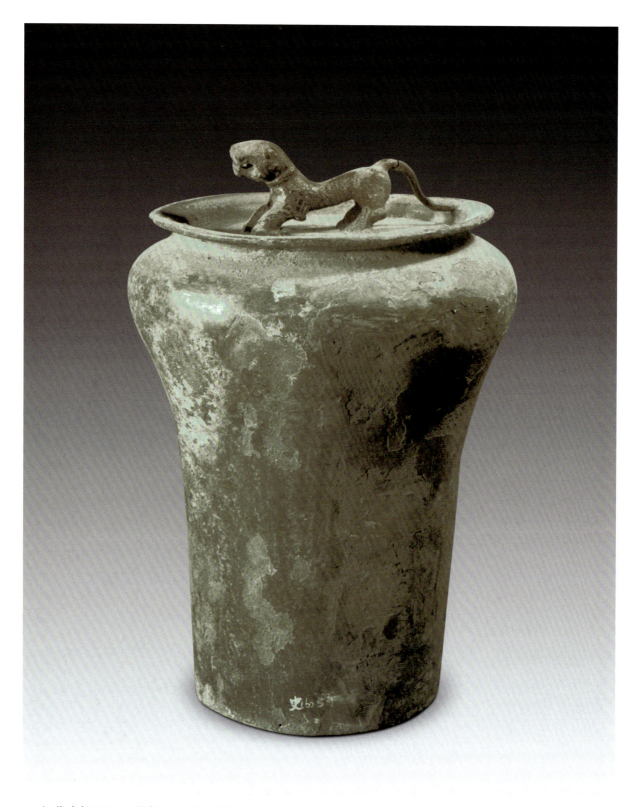

汉代虎钮錞釪　通高 45 厘米　通径 30 厘米
"Huniu Chunyu", ancient bronze percussion instrument, of Han Dynasty
Height, 45 cm; diameter, 30 cm

汉代虎钮錞钎　荆州博物馆提供

"Huniu Chunyu", ancient bronze percussion instrument, of han Dynasty

Provided by Jingzhou Museum

清代四眼铳　通长31厘米
Four-tube blunderbuss of Qing Dynasty
Length, 31 cm

结 束 语
Conclusion

2500 年前产生的《孙子兵法》，代表了中国古代军事思想的最高境界，是东方的大智慧。"自古知兵非好战"，今天我们领会《孙子兵法》的思想精髓，就是要始终不渝地维护世界和平，坚持和平发展，促进人类进步，推动建设持久和平、共同繁荣的和谐世界。

The Art of War written 2500 years ago represents the highest of Chinese ancient military thinking, reflecting the great wisdom of the orient. As history indicates, to study military strategy does not imply the intention to wage war. Today, while we appreciate the essence of the ideas in The Art of War, we will unswervingly maintain world peace, pursue peaceful development, promote the progress of mankind and contribute to building a harmonious world of lasting peace and common prosperity.